INVISIBLE POWERFUL ENERGIES

PSYCHIC CONNECTIONS & SPIRITUAL GROWTH

ARLENE THOMPSON

Note for Librarians: A cataloguing record for this book is available from Library and Archives Canada at www.collectionscanada.ca/amicus/index-e.html

ISBN 1-4120-7242-5

Printed in Victoria, BC, Canada. Printed on paper with minimum 30% recycled fibre. Trafford's print shop runs on "green energy" from solar, wind and other environmentally-friendly power sources.

TRAFFORD
PUBLISHING™

Offices in Canada, USA, Ireland and UK

This book was published *on-demand* in cooperation with Trafford Publishing. On-demand publishing is a unique process and service of making a book available for retail sale to the public taking advantage of on-demand manufacturing and Internet marketing. On-demand publishing includes promotions, retail sales, manufacturing, order fulfilment, accounting and collecting royalties on behalf of the author.

Book sales for North America and international:
Trafford Publishing, 6E–2333 Government St.,
Victoria, BC v8t 4p4 CANADA
phone 250 383 6864 (toll-free 1 888 232 4444)
fax 250 383 6804; email to orders@trafford.com

Book sales in Europe:
Trafford Publishing (uk) Limited, 9 Park End Street, 2nd Floor
Oxford, UK ox1 1hh UNITED KINGDOM
phone 44 (0)1865 722 113 (local rate 0845 230 9601)
facsimile 44 (0)1865 722 868; info.uk@trafford.com

Order online at:
trafford.com/05-2137

10 9 8 7 6 5 4

ARLENE THOMPSON, *R. N., M.H.Sc.,* is the author of *Invisible Powerful Energies, Psychic Connections and Spiritual Growth.* Since the 1960s she has worked as a professional nurse in England and in Canada. Her experience as a direct caregiver has occurred in remote and isolated areas of the High Arctic, on First Nation reservations in Northern Ontario, and in acute care teaching hospitals and community hospitals in South–western Ontario. She has also specialized in cardiac care nursing, and nursing care for adults with acute leukemia, the latter forming the basis for her research in graduate studies. During the past twenty years she held senior administrative positions in hospitals and in the Canadian Council on Health Facilities Accreditation.

Arlene indicates that while her pace and direction have changed in retirement, her interest in helping others remains strong. Her readers will discover the long and sometimes bumpy road she has experienced on her spiritual journey, and she offers this first book to them with the same passion and care that she always felt and gave to her patients. She lives in London, Ontario, Canada.

About the book

An informative and inspiring book, *Invisible Powerful Energies* ensures us that we are capable of hearing our intuition and encourages us to listen closely. In a clear style, Arlene Thompson offers thought-provoking ideas and shares intimate experiences. As stated in the introduction, she has "fully reconciled her past need for privacy with her current desire to openly embrace the world of spirit."

While there is an abundance of books about spiritual awareness and psychic connections, few present the personal thoughts of someone whose extensive career in nursing has closely involved her in the experiences of the dying and grieving. This first book by Arlene, with a full chapter devoted to the true stories of friends and acquaintances, is a fascinating account of *"invisible powerful energies"* that we too can harvest on our own personal journeys.

This book is dedicated to my long-time friend Christine Egan and her brother, Michael Egan, who perished in the destruction of the World Trade Centre by terrorists on September 11, 2001.

Unto Thee, O Lord, do I lift up my soul (Psalm 25:1).

For I am persuaded, that neither death, nor life, nor angels, nor principalities, nor things present, nor things to come, nor height, nor depth, nor any other creature, shall be able to separate us from the love of God, which is in Christ Jesus, our Lord. (Romans 8:38,39).

Remember that love and faith are the strongest links.

CONTENTS

❧

ACKNOWLEDGEMENTS

To Rosemary Powers, my best friend, your generous and continuous support and your patient ear from the conception of this book to its completion and publication is deeply appreciated.

Betty Ann Turpin, your friendship, your interest and your incessant curiosity provided me with inspiration; your comments were always welcomed and greatly appreciated.

My gratitude flows abundantly to my Scottish friend A. Lancaster, "Lanky," for her unswerving interest and wise counsel. Our friendship began in the High Arctic many years ago.

Jennifer Jackman, thank you my friend for your positive contribution to my personal life, your sense of humour, your time for discussions, and your belief in my abilities.

Tony Diodati's friendship and discussions related to the power of silence and personal inner change provided me with a spiritual resource for which I am grateful.

The friendship that I share with my brother Mervyn Thompson is almost a predestined spiritual relationship that has continued to grow over the years. His support is a mainstay in my life.

My sincere appreciation extends to all the friends and acquaintances who contributed their true life experiences; without them, this book would be incomplete.

Thank you to my spirit guides for their constant encouragement.

Thank you to the spiritual mediums for lifting the veil between my physical world and the spiritual realms. Their readings provided me with peace and comfort and they will be forever remembered with love.

Thank you, Jocelyne, for providing me with past life review opportunities and for the spiritual presence you bring into my world. Your support is valued and appreciated.

Pamela Evans, thank you for your continued interest and enthusiastic encouragement.

I have come to rely on my friend and editor, Judy Powers, for without her talented editorial "tough love," this book would never have been published.

Todd J. Thompson, my nephew and friend, thank you for preparing the layout and design. Your talent and the time you provided is greatly appreciated.

I truly believe that the devoted friends with whom I am blessed are a gift from God.

❧

FOREWORD

Even with the scientific and technological advances of today's world we still know relatively little about the influences of psychic phenomena and the power of spiritual mediums. We know however, that there are individuals who appear to possess a sixth sense, a heightened awareness of some spiritual presence, a gift of premonition or an unusual connection to the otherworldly.

I've known Arlene Thompson for over fifteen years. During those years she has frequently engaged me in philosophical conversations about her spiritual and psychic experiences and her interactions with psychic mediums. I have come to believe that she is indeed one of those rare individuals who possess a heightened ability to discern the presence of spirits.

As a physician trained in the art and science of medicine,

I found the idea of psychic phenomena had very little basis in reality. In the years that I've known Arlene however, she has gradually given me a glimpse into her amazing interactions with various mediums and her personal interactions with spirits. I have been enthralled, entertained and, awestruck, enthralled and entertained because Arlene is a wonderful story-teller, in awe because some of the things that she recounted for me could not have happened if there is not a higher spiritual presence or connection with another world through some psychic power.

I have known of Arlene's desire to write of her spiritual and psychic experiences since the early days of our friendship and have listened intently as she told me of her interactions with spiritual mediums, previously unknown to her, who received messages from spirits encouraging her to write. For me, however, the most compelling evidence of some other force in Arlene's world was one particular reading with a spiritual medium.

The medium reminded Arlene of a time when she was ten years old in her grandfather's blacksmith shop. Her grandfather intent on his work with the anvil, inadvertently spit his chewing tobacco on her new oxford saddle shoes. How could the medium possibly have known such a personal piece of information that happened so long ago?

Arlene Thompson is a dedicated healthcare professional and devoted sister and aunt. She is a true and tried friend with a tremendous degree of personal integrity. She has an amazing network of friends and acquaintances from around the world because she is one of the only people I know who makes extraordinary efforts to communicate regularly with many people she has met on her life's journey.

I am delighted that Arlene has fulfilled one of her dreams in writing this book. I believe that you will find it very interesting and enjoyable.

Jennifer Jackman, M.D.

❧

INTRODUCTION

The stories within this book are all true. In some instances, names of individuals have been changed to protect their privacy. In the past, I shared my unfolding awareness of psychic events, spiritual evolution, meditation and my firm belief in the power of prayer with only a few select members of my family and friends. Writing this book required a degree of courage on my part as I have always considered my privacy a priority. Having said that, please know that I have fully reconciled the past need for privacy in favour of openly embracing the mystical world of spirit.

I began to write this book after being told by two different spiritual mediums that spirits informed them that I am to write not one, but actually two books. Initially I thought that I was to finish writing a book of fiction that I had started many years ago. I even found the handwritten draft and read it over to determine whether or not I would complete it. I could not stir sufficient interest or inner motivation to begin the revision of my fictional writing; so I simply ignored the first message from spirit that I was given by a medium in the province of Quebec.

During the interim period of more than one year before I received a reading from a spiritual medium in the province of Ontario, I experienced the following clues which I ignored. On a frequent basis, memories of details about personally experienced psychic phenomena would enter my mind. At some point in each day I would find myself recalling how I first became interested in psychic phenomena and how, over the years, they have impacted my life in many ways. I would often think of the spiritual path I travelled, the meaning of spirituality in my personal life, and the wisdom, peace and self -awareness which assist my continual spiritual evolution. I have come to believe, however, that as part of our humanness, we often simply tune out the inner signals that we receive rather than act on them. The only reason that I can offer is that subconsciously we do not really want to put forth the psychological or emotional effort required in order to respond to the signals.

As you will learn in this book, I then received from spirit a very clear message through a reading provided in Ontario. There was no doubt that I was being guided to write a book about my personal psychic experiences and my personal spiritual journey. I then fully recognized that spirit intended me to write of the sequence of events in my life, in order to help others to "open the door" and feel comfortable about sharing the mystical happenings in their lives. Since that recognition I have discovered a wonderful excitement about embracing new experiences and developed a greater awareness that we are all one in spirit, all a spark of the Divine. I am thankful that I awakened to the opportunity being offered to me and that spirit provides constant guidance.

My story begins when I was a child living in a small town in Ontario, Canada, and spans a period of over fifty years. I share with you my emerging awareness of psychic discernment at the age of ten years. While I really did not understand what was happening, I somehow knew that my experiences were not the kind that one openly talked about; and so the only person I entrusted the information with was my mother.

Being raised within a Christian home, I attended Sunday school and church and while I am grateful for this religious foundation, I realize now that from a young age I was seeking a spiritual truth that, for me, was missing in the traditional religious doctrine. It is my belief that all of us in our own ways will discover our personal spiritual truths and, as part of this writing, I share with you the steps thus far of my journey.

I have for many years been fascinated with the concept of reincarnation. As a child I used to ask my mother, how it can be possible that we have only one life as there is so much to learn and not enough time? Since my past life experiences, I now have a firm belief in reincarnation.

In the chapters which follow, readers are provided with some information related to reincarnation, karma, past lives, meditation, spiritual transformation, prayer, spirit guides and angels; and I include some of my personal thoughts about death and grief. As well, friends and acquaintances have entrusted me with a number of fascinating true stories about psychic phenomena they have experienced and, in some cases, the consequent impact of spiritual transformation within their own lives. Elizabeth, who is a spiritual medium well-known in areas of England, the United States and Canada, offers comments about her discovery of psychic abilities and their influence, which she considers a blessing, on her life. As you turn the pages of this book we all hope that you will sense the love and joy we experienced in preparing it for you.

As a nurse I have been privileged to listen to many patients talk about their near - death experiences. The middle of the night or early morning seemed to be a favourite quiet time for patients to talk openly about such experiences. Also, it was a time when patients would talk with me about seeing the apparition of a loved one and having a sense of being comforted in the midst of distress. The information they shared never failed to impress upon me the love, faith and courage demonstrated by many adults and children to whom I provided nursing care. While this book does not provide personal details concerning individual patients' near- death experiences, I have included some information received from patients. The near-death experiences of my brother and also of colleagues and friends are included for your interest.

Over time I have come to fully appreciate that meditation requires sincere dedication and discipline. Maintenance of such dedication has taught me that attentive listening brings many riches. Meditation provides a way for us to hear intuitive guidance from our Higher Self, (God), while prayer, on the other hand, allows us to actually talk to God; and, please be assured, He hears each of our prayers. I have discovered that He may not answer my prayers in exactly the way I wanted, but He always answers, and, in retrospect, I often realize that He not only replies, but also gives me a spiritual lesson.

My capacity to listen deeply continues to improve and I know that wherever I go, whatever I do, I have around me my guardian angel and many powerful and loving unseen spirits. This significant knowledge never fails to provide me with a sense of joy. I hope that this book awakens your own natural psychic abilities and helps you to be open to God's grace and guidance.

CHAPTER ONE

AWARENESS UNFOLDING

My name is Arlene. I was named by my father, Franklin A. Thompson, who died in 1940 at the age of thirty-four years. He was diagnosed with sub-bacterial endocarditis (inflammation of the lining of his heart). At that time the antibiotics that would be used today were not available and he died within three months of his diagnosis. My mother later told me that whenever Dad was considered well enough to be home from the hospital, he would ask to have me on his bed and we would spend hours together. I seemed to realize he had little strength and my mother related that I was just content to be in his presence. Thinking back, that was probably the only time that I was "on my best behaviour." I was sixteen months old when my dad died.

When I was about ten years old I began to have a strong awareness of my dad's presence. While I did not understand it at the time, I did not question this sense of "knowing." From that time on I always felt protected and reassured by his spiritual presence and love for me. I grew up in the house that my dad built in a small town in Southwestern Ontario, Canada. When I rode my bicycle down our country roads, walked to school or just lay in our large backyard looking at the clouds, lost in thought, I would begin to feel his presence and I would talk to him quietly in my mind. When I held items that belonged to my dad I would inevitably feel a rush of being enveloped by his presence. I cherished those special moments. This sense of his presence continued well into my twenties. Whenever I achieved something or was challenged by something, he was with me either to celebrate or to provide solace and encouragement. After years of reading and gathering information I began to understand that what I experienced is called clairsentience. This term is used to describe what is now thought to be the most common type of intuitive ability, and I have no doubt that this intuitive ability accounts for my having a sense of his presence, a " knowing" that he was with me. I readily share this information with you because if I can help people who may be experiencing clairsentience to understand, accept and not be afraid of their intuitive abilities, then I have partially achieved my purpose in "putting pen to paper." I now fully recognize that being open to our intuition, to psychic guidance, is like acknowledging and accepting a special spiritual gift We too often bypass psychic guidance in favor of attending to egocentric demands. Acting on our intuition is initially difficult to do, but once we make this choice, there is a tremendous sense of relief in knowing that we have placed the power of our lives into the hands of God. I am getting ahead of myself and at this point will continue to share some more information with you about my life.

While this writing is not intended to describe my family or my childhood in detail, I want to make you aware of the positive family relationships which nurtured me. My mother always provided me with unconditional love and was understanding and supportive when I, at the age of ten years, shared with her my "sense of knowing" of my dad's spiritual presence. While sensing spirits was not a topic one would easily consider discussing with others, my mother listened to me with an open mind and over the years shared many of her memories of my dad. She was a superb person with a wonderful personality and, as long as she lived, our home was always one of my favorite places on earth. Although my stepfather was never really a warm family man, he often displayed a good sense of humour and, in my view, he could dance the Charleston better than anyone! My brother was protective, helpful and often a great tease. He was, and is today, a great friend as well as my beloved brother. My maternal grandparents lived in the West and died while I was very young; therefore, neither my brother nor I had the opportunity to develop a relationship with them. My paternal grandparents, however, lived next door to us and they contributed meaningfully toward the development of my brother and me during our formative years and beyond. Our home was a warm and welcoming place and I would often invite friends to dine there and /or to stay the night.

When I was twenty-two years old I heard of two psychic mediums in Brantford, Ontario, who had the gift of communicating with the spirit world. Now I realize that we all have some mediumistic capabilities, with, as mentioned earlier, clairsentience being the most common. Psychic mediums provide a link between our physical world and the spirit world by using clairvoyance, which allows them to see spirits or to see objects shown to them by spirits, and clairaudience, which permits them to hear spirits. Within the following two to three years I saw both of these mediums at separate times. They were truly gifted and were able to validate their gift of communication with spirits by giving me such information as the way my father died, and the way that my stepfather injured his back when he was a young man by jumping off a bridge into the river on a dare. They also provided detailed and accurate descriptions of my mother and brother. In addition, I was told of plans that I had made but not yet shared with anyone. This information and much more left me in no doubt about the abilities of both mediums. On my first visit to them, a friend agreed to accompany me and arranged to have a reading after me. A real skeptic, she was certain that she would disprove Mr. and Mrs. M.'s psychic abilities. My doubting friend went into the room used for consultations/readings and apparently the very first words spoken by Mrs. M. were "Margaret, please sit down and if you like I will pour you a cup of tea." Well, "Margaret" never used her first name as she always preferred a nickname and, in fact, very few people knew that her Christian name was Margaret. The hour she spent with Mrs. M. turned out to be an astonishing experience for her. Mrs. M. was able to validate her gift of being a medium by providing Margaret with information known only to her and to her immediate family, all of whom lived in another country.

Several months later I revisited Mr. M. At that time I was given a photograph to look at. Captured on film were Mr. and Mrs. M. strolling along a street in a typical suburban, middle class neighbourhood. There were some large trees along the sidewalk and amongst the trees I could see four to five faces. Mr. M. asked me to show the photograph to my friend Margaret, who had again accompanied me. She described what she saw and commented that it was a nice photo of Mr. and Mrs. M., but she could not see any of the other faces that were so obvious to me. Mr. M. then told me that I could see the faces because I have an active and strong intuitive sense that I need to develop and trust. He went on to say that the faces are those of spirits in their family who are almost always with him and his wife. Encouraging me to develop my innate psychic and spiritual abilities, Mr. M. suggested that I enroll in a psychic/medium development course in Toronto. My failure to act on Mr. M.'s well-intentioned suggestion was the result of my youth, some fear about this unknown part of myself, and plans which did not include such a serious undertaking. I have always remained interested in psychic phenomena, however, and have other experiences which I will share with you as you read this book.

During one of my appointments with Mrs. M. she told me that I would travel across a very large body of water within two to four years. She also said that, within my first year of being away, my Mother would become very ill but would survive. The only other person with whom I shared this information was the friend had who accompanied me to the appointment in Brantford. I did not tell my Mother about this part of the reading as I did not want to cause her concern, I could not bear the thought of her becoming ill, and, anyway, I had no intention of traveling across a large body of water.

Over the next two to three years I became friends with several people from England. They planned to return there and invited me to go with them. In 1964, following consultation with my family, I decided that I would travel to England and, while there, train as a nurse. Much later I recognized that my journey to England took place during the latter part of the timeframe predicted by Mrs. M.

One evening in England during the spring of 1965, I was walking home from the hospital where I had just completed a twelve hour tour of duty. The route was a very familiar one. As was the custom at the time, I wore my long nurse's cape over my uniform, and neighbors along the street waved to me from their doorsteps and yard. They were always friendly to me and the other nurses who shared my duplex. This particular evening, however, would prove to be astonishingly different. Just as I approached the telephone kiosk about two blocks from my destination, I suddenly heard a booming voice call out, "ARLENE THOMPSON." I stopped in my tracks, momentarily frozen to the spot. I then took a step forward and once again heard the loud voice call out my name. At that point I ran the rest of the way home. Trembling uncontrollably I experienced an intense knowing that something was wrong. This feeling came from deep within me and, although I can not offer any logical explanation for it, this "knowing" was no fleeting spiritual or emotional concept. As unfathomable as it may sound, the total experience is as real and clear to me today, years later, as it was at the time of its happening.

In retrospect, I do not know if I was receiving a telepathic message or experiencing clairaudience for the first time. A telepathic message, or mind–to–mind communication, has been known to occur between close family members or friends. It usually occurs at a time when strong emotions are involved such as love or distress, and the communication may be heard as words, experienced as feelings, or seen as images. Telepathic sensitivity occurs to many people on an almost routine basis. Think of how many times you have thought of someone and then received a letter or telephone call from the person. Also, think of the times that you intuitively know who is calling. Later in this book I will share with you another experience and some additional information about clairaudience.

Two days later my brother unexpectedly arrived from Canada to tell me that our mother was in hospital and diagnosed as having had a heart attack. Because my mother was considered to be out of immediate danger, my brother had chosen to tell me in person rather than by telephone, and an arrangement was speedily made for me to return to Canada. Arriving at the hospital I was relieved to be able to see her and to be with her again. The nurses who were with Mother during her most critical hours shared with me that she often called out my name. I have come to believe that the booming voice I heard in England and the intense knowing that something was wrong was a telepathic message from my mother, or a message from the spirit realm on behalf of my mother. This message, I am certain, was linked to my mother calling my name during her most difficult hours.

During some quiet moments at the hospital while my mother was resting, I recalled what I had been told by Mrs. M. four years earlier. "You will travel across a very large body of water, and during your first year away, your mother will be ill but she will survive." During the intervening years I had forgotten some of what I had been told by Mrs. M., the medium in Brantford. As events unfolded, I began to remember her words in detail and realized the predictions were accurate. I spent seven weeks at home following my Mother's discharge from hospital and we enjoyed the opportunity to talk and share memories, tears and laughter. She heard details about Peter, a man I was dating, as I wanted her to know how much I was beginning to care for him. (In early May, 1966, Peter and I announced our engagement.) This time at home with my mother was very special for us both, but while I was prepared to remain in Canada, my mother insisted that I return to England to finish my training.

During late October, 1965, I woke up in the middle of the night covered in perspiration, trembling and crying, but with clear recall of what I considered to be a nightmare. The dream which I recounted in detail that night to a colleague and friend (one of three who shared the duplex with me) clearly depicted details of my mother's funeral.

This experience was extremely disturbing, and only after many hours of discussion could I begin to accept the idea that concern for my mother's well-being plus the stress of second year exams were the cause.

Travel plans were made for me to return home for a holiday in May, 1966. My mother and I were looking forward to having time together again; however, fate intervened. Five days before I was scheduled to leave England I received a telephone call from my brother to tell me that our mother had just experienced a fatal myocardial infarction. She died at home on May 23. I left for Canada the next day with my fiancé, Peter, on the earliest available flight. After our arrival I discovered that arrangements for Mother's funeral had been organized by my brother and step-father. On the day of my mother's funeral, the events were identical to the ones in my nightmare.

These extraordinary experiences and others since that time have given me "permission" to become more comfortable with the mysteries of our universe. I recognize that happenings in our physical world on earth will not always be explained by acceptable scientific theories. During the time of grief for my mother, I came to realize more fully my quiet faith, my trust in God, and to recognize that He remained with me through that terrible storm of loss in my life. Also, in a large measure, it was at that time that I learned to reaffirm, value and trust my intuition. I now have an insatiable curiosity about and openness to psychic guidance.

Shortly after returning to England for the final year of training, I drove to Scotland with Jane, a friend and colleague. While we were at a bed and breakfast establishment near Edinburgh an interesting incident occurred. Sandy, my friendly Pembrokeshire Corgi, entered the room we had rented and immediately started to growl. The hair on her back rose as she carefully approached an empty corner of the room. On inspection, there was nothing to be seen and the room appeared to Jane and me to be neat, clean and comfortable. We walked outside to investigate the exterior of the house and, finding nothing, returned to the room. We all spent an extremely restless night as Sandy made it quite clear that "something" in the room disturbed her. We related our story to the owners at breakfast the next morning and left with the mystery unsolved. I firmly believe that there was a spirit present in the room that Sandy could sense but we could not.

I made a difficult decision when I returned to England from Canada, and that was to break my engagement to Peter. The next event took place about six weeks after I returned my engagement ring to him. I will relate it to you as accurately as possible. A friend and colleague who shared my duplex joined me on a walk with Sandy to a favourite park not far from where we lived. The park was located near some lovely old streets with large older homes and, as we were walking, we noted a sign on a pole which provided information about a visiting psychic medium from Wales. We decided to return and join the audience at 7:00 p.m. We arrived in time to find seats among approximately 100 people. As I recall, the medium was in her mid-forties, a very animated, attractive woman with thick auburn hair. In her strong Welsh accent, she began to address some members in the group and provided them with messages from spirits. I was taken by surprise when she asked me if I would mind if she gave me a message that was very personal. After a fleeting moment of hesitation, as indeed this "personal message" would be heard by the whole audience, I succumbed to my curiosity and told her to go ahead. She then proceeded to say, "I am being asked by spirit to let you know that returning the engagement ring about six weeks ago was the right decision to make and that you must not worry about it, just let it go." Imagine my astonishment at the time and my recognition of yet another demonstration of clairvoyance. As I reflect on some events in my life, it seems to me that I required many demonstrations to erase my lingering doubt about the ability of individuals to be highly intuitive.

Another event that I must share with you also occurred while I was a student nurse in England. I heard from the various staff and senior students about a nursing sister (supervisor/coordinator is the more common title in North America) who died while on duty. They told me that her spirit continues to "make rounds" to see that all is well. It was near the end of my second year when I had the following experience. Another nurse and I were on duty on a female medical ward. At that time, men and women were cared for on separate wards/units and we rotated in training to the various female and male medical and surgical wards. We asked the nursing sister on night duty to bring us a particular medication from the pharmacy that we did not usually keep in stock on our ward. We were located on the fourth floor; the stairway to the fifth floor was just to the left, but basically across from our main office. To the right of the office door was an elevator, the old type with a cage-like door, which always creaked loudly with age and rebellion at still having to work. As I walked out of the office I saw the back of a person walking up the stairs; she was wearing the navy blue and white uniform that was traditional for nursing sisters at our hospital. I concluded that there must be an urgent need for her to go directly to the fifth floor, which contained a male medical unit, and that she would stop in on her return down the stairs. I mentioned this assumption to the senior nurse on duty with me. After forty-five minutes passed, she said to me, "Nurse Thompson, please run upstairs and retrieve the medication from Sister as there must be something serious going on that is taking so much of her time." I ran up the stairway and asked one of the nurses what Sister was doing and where I could find her as we needed the medication that we had requested from her. The nurse stated, "Sister has not arrived yet to conduct rounds." When I told her what I had seen, she said that it must have been the apparition of the Sister who had died on duty several years ago. I returned to my ward and shared what I had been told with my colleague. She telephoned Sister and left a message to contact us as soon as possible. As it turned out, Sister arrived within minutes on the creaky old elevator with the medication that we required. She apologized for taking an unusual amount of time to arrive and explained that emergency surgery for a patient had required her to contact the operating room staff on call. When we told her my story, her response was "Not to worry; most of the nurses eventually see the apparition of Sister X doing her rounds."

It was many years later that I began to experience other psychic phenomena. During the intervening years I focused on my career, graduate studies, personal relationships, and time with family and friends here in Canada, America, and the United Kingdom. Nevertheless, more extraordinary occurrences would later affect my life and confirm my belief in intuitive understanding.

CHAPTER TWO

❦

SPIRIT WHISPERS

After nearly twenty years without any memorable psychic experiences, it was during 1985 that I learned through some colleagues about a well-respected medium living in Southwestern Ontario. Her name is Elizabeth and since I had never come across anyone as gifted as Mr. and Mrs. M., I decided to contact her. I telephoned Elizabeth from a pay telephone. I did not offer my name or other personal information, but did make an appointment to see her at her home on a particular evening at 7:00 p.m. She asked me to write down three names of people either living or "passed on to the spirit realm," to fold the paper and to bring it with me. She also asked me to think of two wishes in preparation for our meeting. At the agreed upon time, I arrived to find a very pleasant woman in her mid to late forties. I sat across from her at her desk and she invited me to put the folded paper on the desk, but not to open it. It was never opened and when I left that evening the paper was back in my pocket. Elizabeth told me that the messages she receives are from spirits, that she is simply the medium who conveys the messages. Then she bowed her head in prayer to God and asked for protection against evil. After a short silence, she connected to her spirit guide. Next Elizabeth began to tell me about the many spirits in the room; she had to ask them to speak one at a time as they all had something to say. I will not go into every moment of this experience, but will share some of the details with you.

My mother was the first to enter in spirit and Elizabeth validated her presence by accurately stating to me that Mom had died suddenly of a heart attack. Elizabeth continued by saying, "Arlene, your mother says that she is often with you wherever you are and that she likes your home." She went on to describe "looking out the window of the front door and seeing a large, green hedge across the road and also two large blue spruce trees on either side of the front walkway to the house." Elizabeth conveyed to me my mom's message that she is often with me at night when I read before I go to sleep and she described in detail the blue and white comforter on my bed, even its scalloped edges.   There was much more, all of it comforting and reassuring to me, and, without question, the messages validated my mother's presence in spirit.

Some other messages from the spirit world that were

conveyed to me through Elizabeth included one from my paternal grandfather. She said, "He is asking me to tell you about the time when you were ten years of age and arrived at his blacksmith shop to show him your new saddle shoes. Preoccupied with forging some new horseshoes, he did not notice you standing nearby and when he spat tobacco juice, it landed on one of your new shoes." He told that story to Elizabeth to validate his presence in spirit. No one except my immediate family had known of the incident. I remembered leaving his blacksmith shop horrified that my new shoes had been ruined as, indeed, the stain remained. Loving my grandfather, however, made it easy to forgive him.

The father of a very dear friend had died just a few weeks before my visit to Elizabeth. He confirmed his presence by describing what he termed "his favorite place on earth, a cottage in Northern Ontario." I had visited the cottage a number of times and his description, through Elizabeth, included accurate details about both the inside and outside of the cottage. He also provided her with his first name and gave me a personal message which further validated his presence. Another message came through from the mother and aunt of a good friend. Elizabeth stated, "They want you to let your friend know that her sister will be going into her local hospital emergency, she will have leads put on her chest (an electrocardiogram) and will be admitted for investigation." Elizabeth continued, "They stressed that it may take a very long time to control her blood pressure, but that eventually she will recover." Within the same week of my receiving this information, my friend learned that her sister was taken to emergency in the local hospital, had an electrocardiogram as well as other tests, and was retained for observation. The message given proved to be absolutely correct.

In all instances of receiving messages from spirits, I found it extremely comforting to know that those we love are still with us, are aware of events in our lives, often provide support in our quiet moments and always surround us with love. During that first meeting with Elizabeth I received many messages from family and friends. That so many details remain clear all these years later never fails to amaze me, as sometimes I have difficulty remembering the birthday of a friend or what I did last Monday. The meeting with Elizabeth inspired me to read every book related to psychic phenomena that I could find. Mr. and Mrs. M. had suggested to me years ago that I need to trust my intuition and begin to develop my psychic abilities. My personal quest to seek a greater understanding about these subjects began in earnest.

Later in the 1980s several happenings further increased my interest in psychic phenomena. One day as I was washing my car in my driveway, I went into the house to retrieve something. Coming back outside I saw, just at the side of the house, an apparition resembling my paternal grandfather. The apparition appeared and vanished in a split second, but the memory of it has stayed with me ever since. By this time in my life I had spent a lot of my private hours reading about paranormal happenings, meditation, karma, reincarnation and intuition; so, although I was surprised, not for a moment did I doubt what I had witnessed. I was absolutely delighted that he was so close to me. During my years of working as a nurse, some dying patients indicated to me that they saw by their beds deceased family members. In every instance the experience provided the patient with comfort. However, as witnessed by me, apparitions of the dead are not limited to dying people. Today, I am fully aware that, although we may not see them, our loved ones who have passed to the spiritual realm are always with us.

The following is another event that I want to share with you. You may have trouble believing what I am about to tell you, but, I assure you, it happened as stated. One lovely summer day I was sitting in the kitchen with the windows open, enjoying the slight breeze and fresh air, reading the paper and sipping a cup of coffee. My Siamese cat, Rampa, was sitting in the kitchen with me and had just finished eating her breakfast. Glancing up, I saw, coming towards us from the dining room, two adult raccoons. In amazement, I grabbed Rampa to protect her and ran to the living room where I quickly closed the doors. After listening for some noise and hearing nothing, I carefully walked out of the living room to investigate, but found no trace of the animals. I was somewhat shaken by the event. Later that same day, a friend and colleague who shared my home telephoned to say that as she was preparing to leave for work , she looked out the window and saw two adult raccoons walking across our lawn. She had considered waking me up as she knows how much I love to see wild creatures. (I was known to protect a local groundhog that was often in our backyard.) I then related my experience to her as described above and her response was one of incredulousness. Following this conversation, I telephoned Elizabeth to share the events with her and to ask her opinion. In her view, there were two possible explanations: in a relaxed state in my kitchen, I probably had a heightened intuitive awareness and was able to create an image of the raccoons; or, I had received a telepathic message. To date, that experience has happened to me only that one time. I am not certain of the significance of the unusual incident, but perhaps one day it will be revealed to me.

My interest in psychic phenomena, the afterlife, spiritual realms, reincarnation, and near-death experiences intensified and I immersed myself in reading about the many different religious beliefs and cultural traditions concerning the soul's survival. At this time I also began an earnest exploration of acknowledging and following my intuitive prompting. I have discovered that this investigation requires sincere and dedicated practice which is enhanced by a concerted growth in self-awareness and trust.

At this same time, during the mid to late 1980s, I began to often "feel" the presence of spirits in my home This feeling would occur in any room but was more frequent in the living room. Each experience occurred when my upper body and head felt cold and were covered in goosebumps. This physical manifestation preceded every time that I knew I was being visited by spirits and continues to do so to this day. The only spirit that I was able to identify with any degree of confidence at that time was that of my mother. While I could sense other spirits I could not identify them, but did recognize that they were friendly as I felt comfortable and secure in their presence, not afraid. I often talked of these incidents with my housemate and was able to assure her that there was no need for concern. Indeed there was never any uneasiness. In fact, visitors found our home to be warm and welcoming and, on more than one occasion over the years, we had offers from potential buyers who found our home to be, in their words, "charming and friendly."

In 1986 my professional career in the health care industry took me to Ottawa. A friend there, in anticipation of my arrival, found an apartment quite suitable for me. She was driving through a well-established neighborhood and noticed an advertisement on the lawn of a house. As it turned out, this was the original home of a family but was currently being used by family members for an office, and so they were there only during business hours and the occasional evening or weekend when deadlines would loom. The private entrance to the second floor apartment led to a large landing, a dining room, office area, kitchen and living room. On the third floor, there were two spacious bedrooms. The kitchen was at the back of the house where there was an exit and a small laundry area. This accommodation was, for me, a perfect place. During the three years that I lived there, I was to realize that I had much more to learn about the depth of my intuition and psychic experiences.

In the evening, after dinner, I would often work at my desk. There was a large window directly in front of me and I found it a comfortable place to do what sometimes seemed like endless reviews of reports. The kitchen was two steps away and it was in the kitchen, whenever I went in to refill my cup of coffee, that I began to be aware of the presence of a spiritual entity. My arms, neck and head would often be covered in goosebumps and I would sense a presence with me, an unknown visitor. When my curiosity finally got to me one evening and I telephoned Elizabeth to tell her of my repeated experiences of sensing an unknown spirit, she described the entity in detail including hair style and favourite clothes. It seemed fantastic, for Elizabeth seemed to be painting a picture with words of my paternal grandmother. To realize that she was often near filled me with a pervasive sense of peace. My grandmother's spirit continues to visit me and I always welcome her presence.

Another experience in Ottawa, however, was initially terrifying! One night I was particularly tired and went to my bedroom on the third floor earlier than usual. As is my habit, I read for awhile and then fell asleep. Sometime later I woke up to the pressure of a hand on my left thigh. Fearing that someone had invaded my home, I remember feigning sleep at that point and feeling very frightened. The hand pressure remained. I threw off the covers, jumped out of bed in a flash and raced down the stairs. I heard no one come after me and I could still feel the pressure on my leg. I put on every light in the house, went back upstairs and searched both bedrooms thoroughly. Everything was in good order and so I went back downstairs. Still shaking, I paced the floor trying to settle down. At 3:00 a.m. I did not want to telephone friends who, like myself, had to get up and go to work in the morning. For the rest of the night and for more than ten days, I consistently felt the pressure of a hand on my left thigh. While away on business, I slept in my hotel room with the light on. I have never again experienced the same or a similar happening. I did eventually talk to Elizabeth about it and between us we speculated about the reason for my unseen visitor, but did not come to an absolute conclusion. As I write this, more than a decade later, I am still fully aware of the exact area of my thigh where I felt the pressure.

About six months after the mysterious "visit," I learned of the death of a man who had been raised in the house and who had worked in the offices on the ground floor. He had been an attractive, likeable man in his forties and his presence would be missed by all who knew him, especially his family. That same night, I awoke from a deep sleep and put on my bedside light to see the time. Just before I could put the light off again, I saw an apparition on my other pillow, a face and head which clearly resembled the man who had just died. This sight did not evoke a sense of fear in me, but rather curiosity. As a boy and young man, had he occupied this bedroom and was his spirit paying a visit?

During my time in Ottawa I was introduced to Jocelyne, an individual who is well- known and respected as a regression therapist. Jocelyne now lives in Victoria, British Columbia, and we continue to be in contact. Through her I have learned that regression therapy is not intended merely to satisfy curiosity, but to achieve a particular purpose. Through discussions with Jocelyne I have gained considerable insight into the concept of regression therapy and developed a rapport with her and a high degree of trust in her knowledge, motivation to help others, and her abilities. Therefore, with anticipation rather than any fear of the unknown, I attended my first past life regression. Jocelyne's well-organized and comfortable office was on the second floor of her home. After some preliminary conversation she invited me to lie down, she put a pillow under my head and covered me with a warm blanket. Jocelyne explained that sometimes when experiencing past life regressions, clients may feel really cold in response to memories accessed that are fearful. She then placed a scarf over my eyes to help me focus within, encouraged me to relax, and in a few moments, whenever I felt ready, she would begin to guide me toward a past life. When I signalled to her that I was ready to begin this new journey, she instructed me to visualize a staircase, any kind of staircase I would like. It could be old and rickety, or beautiful marble or oak, whatever I preferred. When I told her that I was able to "see" a staircase of my choosing, she asked me to visualize a door at the bottom of the staircase; the door could be of my choosing, simple and light, or ornate and heavy, or any other way that I wished it to be. I then counted myself down the stairs, beginning with ten, as I visualized descending them. When I reached the bottom, I was to open the door and step through to a past life. At first, I could not open the door and I told Jocelyne that I was unable to open it. She responded in a calm, quiet voice that I should just take my time, that when I was ready I would be successful. To my amazement I did open the door and walked through it to find myself dressed in the federal American cavalry uniform of the mid 1800s. When Jocelyn asked me to describe what I was wearing from the feet up, I told her of my uniform. She then asked me to describe my surroundings and I told her that I was in a busy fort and that I could hear the sounds of horses and men and the smell of horses, and leather boots and saddles. In the distance some rations were being cooked on an open fire. I was not sure what my rank was, but I did know that I was the senior person responsible for the men who were preparing to engage in fighting. Of great concern to me were the young recruits, the men sent to replace others who had died. When I sent a messenger to the command post, which was a day's ride away, to ask for more training time for the new men, I was told that it would not be possible and that I must continue with the planned orders. With a heavy heart I sent the men on a mission that would cost many lives. I felt a tremendous responsibility for the deaths of so many. Sometime later I was also mortally wounded, but able to relate vividly details of my injuries and to describe the person who was with me offering solace at the time of my death. Since my first past life experience, I now have a greater appreciation and understanding of the factors that may have contributed to an overwhelming sense of duty and responsibility for others during my current lifetime. This innate and overpowering sense of obligation, combined with my naturally strong empathetic sense, has created a number of important personal challenges. While I admit to some continuing inner struggle, I recognize that I am not responsible for everyone around me, but rather that I am responsible for myself and my own interpretation of events, whether they are negative or positive in nature.

Another past life regression found me walking through an area that was like a bayou. There were a few tall, slim trees and shafts of sunlight seemed to dance through them. I felt comfortable as this area was home to me and I had the distinct feeling that the time period was during the early 1900s. I was a seventeen–year-old male wearing a new shirt made by my mother, my Sunday trousers and my only pair of shoes.

I was very happy; I jingled some change in my pocket, whistled, walked quickly and daydreamed about the girl I would meet in town. Suddenly a large alligator charged from the edge of a pond, grabbed my upper leg and hip, dragged me into the water, and tore off a large chunk of flesh. At the time of the attack I literally yelled out in fear and pain and sat straight up throwing the blanket off and grabbing my legs. Jocelyne quickly assured me that I was all right and could continue to relive this past life and describe the events as I experienced them. I then said quietly to her, "An alligator has bitten into my leg, I am being dragged into a pond and the pond is turning red with my blood. I cannot get away; I just cannot get away and I am trying to claw my way up a muddy slippery embankment." I went on to describe my desperation and fear of the alligator and my pleas to God for help. Just before my death I called out to God, "Why now? Why me? I don't want to die now. Please help me." Then I could see my body slip away into the pond and, in a sense, I traded pain and fear for peace. Jocelyne helped me to relive this traumatic experience when I died in devastating shock which prevented me from fully reconnecting to my spirit. Reliving this experience allowed me to come to terms with my death: by making it conscious, I was able to allow spiritual energy to flow into this part of my soul.

Immediately following this regression when Jocelyne and I talked at length, I remembered an incident in my current lifetime. I shared with Jocelyn that when I was seventeen–years-old I worked during the summer at a psychiatric facility and lived in the residence which was located across the road. One lovely summer morning I was walking on the sidewalk through the beautifully manicured grounds on my way to work, lost in thought about Ron, a very special fellow I had been out with the night before. Suddenly, I felt a searing pain in my left hip. The intensity of it stopped me in my tracks. To resume walking required supreme effort and by the time I entered my place of work I was hanging onto the wall to keep myself steady and upright. After I rested for awhile, the pain subsided to a bearable degree, but when I tried to attend to some of the patients, I quickly discovered that I could not walk without excruciating pain. An ambulance was called and I was transported to the local community hospital where I remained as a patient for over two weeks. I received many x-rays and heat lamp treatments, bedrest for a week, and an oral treatment of muscle relaxants plus other pain control medications. In the end I was discharged without a definitive diagnosis and spent the next four weeks slowly attempting to regain a level of acceptable physical activity without the associated pain. From that time until my late forties when I experienced the past life regression that I have described, severe pain in my hip and leg occurred every year, and for at least one to two days I would have to put myself on a treatment of bedrest and muscle relaxants in order to resume my normal activity. Jocelyne talked to me about soul memory: the soul retains all memory of the spiritual world. Healing can occur through past life regression such as I had experienced, and since then my conscious understanding of what had happened to me in a previous life allowed me to acknowledge the pain when it occurred again and request it to leave me. Twice I felt the old familiar pain and twice I requested it to leave and I have never had the pain again.

Over time, I experienced three other past lives and each of them contributed in some measure toward a greater understanding of myself and my relationships in my current life. One past life took place in Rome where I was a member of the Praetorian Guard. In another, I was a female school teacher in a small town in the Mid-western United States, and in another, I was a "gentleman of means"; both of these latter experiences seemed to take place in the 1800s. In all instances of past life regression, I recall the details with astounding clarity.

To write about the psychic experiences in my life requires a degree of courage while at the same time, in a way, allows me to be totally myself. This admission also sets me apart because, while we are all psychic, we are not all receptive to the energy systems and vibrations that enable one to perceive intuitive guidance toward spiritual growth and understanding. Having said that, I need also to say that I consider myself a learner with an open and objective mind.

▼

CHAPTER THREE

❧

Spiritual Energies

y own personal quest towards psychic and spiritual understanding has led me to investigate a number of relevant topics. Many people have written at length about the following subjects; so, it is not my intention to delve deeply into them but rather to provide you with some "food for thought" which may encourage you to seek more information.

Reincarnation

There are various divergent religious and cultural beliefs about the soul's survival after physical death. Many of the Christians whom I know question the validity of reincarnation, the belief that our soul or spirit returns to a physical body on earth in order to continue to evolve through diverse learning experiences before attaining a constant presence with God in the spiritual realms. Christians do believe, however, that after physical death we exist as souls in "heaven or hell." There are many biblical texts, such as the following one, that support such a belief: "For I say unto you, that except your righteousness shall exceed the righteousness of the scribes and the Pharisees, ye shall in no case enter into the Kingdom Of Heaven" (Matthew 5:20).

In contrast, Tibetan Buddhists are numbered among the religious cultures that believe in reincarnation. Recently a friend sent me information about the Dalai Lama, the exiled spiritual leader of the Tibetan people. My friend also indicated that she participates in a discussion group at her Protestant church; the focus for the next discussion will be related to the wise comments and spiritual beliefs that the Dalai Lama talked about during his 2004 visit to Canada. This step by the Protestant church members toward a greater understanding of another quite different religious culture is commendable.

Experiences such as near-death episodes, apparitions of the dead and past life memories support the notion that our ongoing evolution beyond life as we now know it is just a part of our spiritual journey. As you know through reading the previous chapters of this book, many experiences in my life have directed me to a belief in reincarnation. From time to time during an informal gathering, I ask people for their views on the subject, and on each occasion, without fail, there are some others who also believe in reincarnation.

On a day–to-day, life-to-life basis, I am convinced that lessons are given to us and that we are to master these lessons to make room for more learning. Because of my personal experience of regression into past lives, it is reasonable and feasible for me to maintain to myself and to others that reincarnation allows our souls to evolve. The constant cycle of births and deaths involving a series of bodies allows us to encounter all the spiritual lessons that can be learned only through the totality of all experiences. It seems logical that in each lifetime there are certain lessons to learn and that, as we evolve, we become spiritually more advanced. The process, then, is one of continual progression.

The key is love; God is the light of pure love and we must remember that the purpose of each of our lives is to grow in the ability to love. Life is truly choice and learning to choose love as you live each moment is not an easy task. Consider one day of your life in which you choose to live each moment with love. A typical day for me tests my patience when, for example, a friend wants to tell me all that has "gone wrong" with his/her day, or when the numerous telephone calls from people asking for donations to charities interrupt my writing. Love means opening yourself to the power of forgiving, forgiving yourself and others and caring for others despite personal hurts. It is a greater challenge to forgive than to hold a grudge and feel bitterness, for the act of forgiveness must be shown in a generous and gentle manner. I truly believe that seeking the grace of forgiveness is essential for spiritual growth.

To me the concept of reincarnation implies a yearning to reach within to find your true self. The cycle of births and deaths allows us to begin to understand our world on earth which was created by God. Consider the tiny role we each have in just one physical lifetime; then imagine having numerous opportunities to acquire the lessons learned from the experiences of many lifetimes. Their circumstances will vary. One life may present wealth; another, poverty; one, fame; another obscurity. One's sex and sexual orientation may change from life to life. One may play a variety of roles: mother, father, daughter, son, teacher, caregiver, scientist or politician. Diverse experiences allow us to learn about life from every vantage point and we will know failures, successes, mistakes, tragedy, humility and love.

In truth, everything we are or have is a gift from God. How we manage what we have and the lessons that are given to us is, in my view, a reflection of our level of spiritual growth and our relationship with God. Think about how important it is to get to know someone, either someone you are in love with, or someone you would like to befriend. You commit yourself to learning about the other through spending time together, for, if you do not, then your relationship, despite the best of intentions, will turn out to be quite superficial and, chances are, it will not survive. On the other hand, the relationships that we nurture, particularly the ones in which we recognize and accept our differences, may well last for a lifetime.

It is reasonable to believe that as sparks of the Divine created by God, we are all connected, despite being different from each other in countless ways. As we evolve in our individual journeys to our ultimate destiny we are able to see clearly the evidence of our spiritual growth. That development is simply not possible, and to the thoughtful mind was never meant to be possible, in one lifetime. We are here because we have been here before, and each of us is now in this current lifetime preparing for our next reincarnation.

It is, I believe, a misconception to think that we immediately reincarnate after physical death. It is of value, regardless of how time is measured, to keep in mind that the ultimate goal is not simply to reincarnate but rather to move forward spiritually, and it is this action that is the purpose of reincarnation. We are not here by chance; coincidence does not exist. We are here as part of an inevitable process, a well-developed intelligent plan. Logical reasoning clearly indicates that one lifetime is absolutely insufficient. We are an intrinsic part of the Divine, connected to each other and to God. It is meaningless to even consider that we simply appear on earth for one life. Think of it; how could we possibly advance the evolution of our imperfect spirits in one lifetime? In this lifetime we are preparing our destiny for our next life and what we sow, we also will reap. We are here to serve God and to continue to grow spiritually. We serve God by doing everything out of love, even the smallest act of kindness to brighten someone else's day. It is, though, important to bear in mind that it is not so much what we do, but what we intend to do. We must strive for what is good and right, for what contributes to the fulfillment of our divine purpose and the development of our spiritual growth.

Biblical Texts that Suggest Support for Reincarnation

The first text addresses the identity of John the Baptist. Jesus says, "And if ye will receive it, this is E-li'as, (John the Baptist), which was for to come" (Matthew 11:14). In the same gospel, while answering his disciples about the coming of E-li'as, Jesus replies, "But I say unto you, that E-li'as is come already, and they knew him not, but have done unto him whatsoever they listed. Likewise shall also the Son of man suffer of them." The next verse states: "Then the disciples understood that he spake unto them of John the Baptist(Matthew 17:12-13)." These verses seem to suggest the reincarnation of the prophet E-li'as as John the Baptist.

The prophet Malachi foretells the mission of John the Baptist and the coming of the Lord: "Behold, I will send my messenger and he shall prepare the way before me: and the Lord, whom ye seek, shall suddenly come to his temple, even the messenger of the covenant, whom ye delight in: behold, he shall come, saith the Lord of hosts" (Malachi 3: 1).

The Gospel according to St. Luke announces the birth of John the Baptist: "But the angel said unto him, Fear not Zacharias: for thy prayer is heard; and thy wife Elisabeth shall bear thee a son and thou shalt call his name John" (Luke 1: 13). The angel says, "And he shall go before him in the spirit and power of E-li'as to turn the hearts of the fathers to the children, and the disobedient to the wisdom of the just; to make ready a people prepared for the Lord" (Luke 1: 17). The words "in the spirit and power of E-li'as" lead one to believe that John the Baptist was the reincarnation of E-li'as. When John the Baptist began his public ministry, the priests in Jerusalem questioned his identity as recorded in John1: 21: "And they asked him, What then? Art thou E-li'as? And he saith, I am not. Art thou that prophet? And he answered, no." His response suggests another meaning to the words "in the spirit and power of E-li'as." It is possible that John the Baptist denied being E-li'as because although he carried the living spirit of the prophet, he did not have access to E-li'as's personal physical memories. As noted earlier, in Matthew,11: 14 Jesus said in the plainest possible way, "And if thee will receive it, this is E-li'as, which was for to come." He adds, "He that hath ears to hear, let him hear (Matthew 11: 15). We know that as E-li'as did, so too did John the Baptist have to suffer persecution and, like the prophet E-li'as, he too had a spiritual mission.

For readers who wish to learn more about the doctrine of reincarnation as taught by early Christians I will provide a list of suggested reading. The ancient teachings about the pre-existence of the soul and reincarnation are worthy of intelligent and thoughtful inquiry. For instance, Origen, the great father of the early church,(c.185 - c.254), was the first person after Paul to develop a system of theology around the teachings of Jesus

Origen also believed in reincarnation.

Karma

The Canadian Edition of Funk and Wagnells Standard College Dictionary provides this definition of "karma": "In Buddhism and Hinduism, the doctrine of responsibility for all one's acts in all incarnations that explains. and justifies good and evil fortune. Loosely; fate or destiny." After everything that I have read and discussed with other people about karma, it is, I believe, important to ensure that compassion for others is authentic and sincere if we wish our actions to be viewed as positive karma. We must not try to enhance our egos by our actions, but truly have the best of intentions to create good for others. I think the most positive karma comes from the personal motivation to alleviate the suffering of others and this ability is definitely enhanced if the drive is motivated by compassion rather than obligation.

Several passages of the Bible relate to karma:

"Judge not, that ye not be judged. For with what judgement ye judge, ye shall be judged: and with what measure ye mete, it shall be measured to you again" (Matthew 7: 1-2). "....whatsoever ye would that men should do to you, do ye even so to them: for this is the law and the prophets" (Matthew 7:12). "Take heed that you despise not one of these little ones; for I say unto you that in heaven their angels do always behold the face of my Father which is in heaven" (Matthew18:10). "Then said Jesus unto him, Put up again thy sword into his place: for all they that take the sword shall perish with the sword" (Matthew 26: 52).

"Be not deceived: God is not mocked; for whatsoever a man soweth, that too shall he also reap" (Galatians, verses: 6-7).

The idea is that all things balance out over different incarnations. Balance, however, is only one part of karma; the other part involves soul evolution. Some of us seem to learn our lessons more quickly than others, and there is little doubt in my mind that we have lots of opportunities to continue our learning and spiritual growth through numerous physical lifetimes.

Past Lives

Past life regression is unequivocally linked to the concept of reincarnation and, as I described earlier, during a personal past life regression experience, I was healed of a physical problem that I had endured for many years. I remain in awe of the therapeutic value achieved. There are numerous behaviours exhibited by people in current incarnations that can be traced back to prior lifetimes. For example, fear of water in one's present life can result from a past life drowning; similarly, a man I know cannot tolerate anything around his neck, for he believes that in centuries past, he was beheaded.

Other evidence supports the belief in past lives. For example, spontaneous experiences by children of past lives and reincarnation are well researched and documented by Dr. Ian Stevenson, a medical physician whose work in this area is known to be accomplished through stringent methodology and attention to detail. For those of you who wish to read in depth about Dr Stevenson's research, references will be provided in the suggested reading list.

Sometimes an individual will have an inexplicable interest in a particular historical event, a language or an area of the world. Sometimes a person is able to master a new skill as if he already knew it. When I was a teenager, I would create complex mathematical quizzes to challenge my brother. After receiving a few instructions, he would work out the problem in his mind and answer correctly within moments. It was and continues to be an amazing ability of his. Such a feat may be a first clue to a past life.

Commonplace occurrences also provide evidence of a previous existence. When meeting someone for the first time, or walking down a street in a city not previously visited, you may have experienced a sense of familiarity. A feeling of comfort, a "knowing" may linger with you or even overwhelm you. In such instances, you are likely catching a glimpse of a past life. Similarly, we sometimes meet people that we immediately bond with, are very comfortable with, or, for some unknown reason, do not like. Probably such individuals were in some way associated with us in a past life.

Unresolved issues from the past may be reactivated in a current lifetime and such issues may be the result of traumatic events. Regression therapy is sometimes used to help resolve experiences which may be blocking one's progress in a present incarnation.. Certainly I do not mean to imply that all the problems we encounter are from previous lifetimes; nevertheless, past life therapy has been used to help people suffering from phobias, an intense and unnatural fear of death and long-standing interpersonal difficulties and, as in my own case, a physical problem. It is my understanding that past life regression is also thought to be beneficial for accessing past life accomplishments and strengths.   Re-experiencing such positive achievements could enhance a person's self confidence and enable him to deal with current lifetime difficulties.

Meditation

My first attempt to meditate was in the mid 1980s when I lived in Ottawa. I am sure you are not surprised by that information because you now know that many other interesting happenings occurred to me while I lived there. I was not very good at meditating in the early years, for while I could learn the various techniques, I would often fall asleep. I have since learned that being able to listen to my inner voice, my connection to God within, takes practice and dedication. We are so "caught up" in our materialistic world and global events that it is far from easy to find periods of silence and contemplation; however, when we discover the joy of silence, we also find it possible to turn our attention inward and to understand and value the moment, to truly value living in the now.

Moreover, developing a high level of inner awareness encourages mindfulness of our surroundings.

When I was living and working in remote reservations in Northern Ontario, I made house visits by boat, skidoo or walking. During the latter I noticed that deer, moose, and other creatures have a place to conceal themselves at times during the day. They seek this "quiet corner" and enjoy the cool of the shade as a means of obtaining a solitary retreat. So, too, we must choose some place and time every day for retiring and recreating ourselves, for achieving a protection from the storms of life. I have come to realize that I must be still; I must meditate. This requirement is an essential part of my spiritual path and the spiritual growth that I seek. Through the practice of meditation and deep concentration I am learning to discard my attachments to our physical/material world in favour of deeper insight and understanding of the Christ within. Trusting intuitive guidance means letting go and truly placing your life in God's care. I recall a particular gentleman whom I always held in high esteem saying to me, "Whenever you struggle with a life-changing decision, you should let go- and let God." That message is now a part of my personal support system and an oft – repeated reminder to let God take over each moment of my life.

Meditation becomes increasingly appealing as inner development begins and is strengthened . Kindness to self and to others, love for all of God's creation and developing a sense of calmness and peace are essential ingredients towards acceptance of meditation as a natural process. There are some helpful books available to anyone wishing to learn the art of meditation and I will include some titles on the suggested reading list. One word of caution: it is important that you develop your capacity for meditation at a speed that is comfortable for you. Daily practice is important, but the length of time will vary for each individual.

Spiritual Transformation

In the *What is Enlightenment Magazine,* an article entitled "A Philosopher of Change" is the result of an interview with Yasuhilo Kimura, the Japanese–American author of *Think Kosmically Act Globally.* While he does not profess to be a spiritual teacher, he states: "Transformation is a movement that is primarily from being to becoming, into creating." Throughout our lives we read books, experience events, listen to other viewpoints, and over time we gain a comprehensive body of knowledge. Recognizing and accepting our intuition then allows us to incorporate this extensive information into our own understanding and the process of transformation begins to take place.

The first clue about spiritual transformation was provided to me in the 1960s when I lived in the High Arctic. It has taken me many years to come to my present understanding of spirituality. A wealth of subtle evidence occurred along the way but some were recognized only in retrospect. When you stop seeing things in a strictly material/physical way, then it becomes possible to recognize the pattern of events, and to begin to understand why things happen as they do. There is a master plan, and as I have stated many times, there is no such thing as coincidence, no chance encounters. There is a purpose for all that comes to each of us in this life and, therefore, many opportunities, many clues to locate the path to spiritual transformation. Take some time to reflect on the people in your life who have influenced you, on the relationships, whether short– lived or enduring, on the hurt, joy and lessons learned. Through such personal reflection you will know, beyond any doubt, that no one is in your life by accident. Even brief encounters have a significant purpose, for there are lessons to be learned each step along your journey. Your biological family, your friends, colleagues, lovers, and, yes, even individuals you would prefer not to know are a necessary part of your life to help you attain your full potential in spiritual growth. When you let go of self-centredness and develop a new insight as the result of consciously returning to the source of your being, then it becomes possible to combine your new insight with your present body of knowledge and transformation begins.

Prayer

Sincere, heartfelt prayer is the most powerful form of energy that one can generate, and the results of such prayer can often be measured in greater moral stamina and a deeper understanding of the realities underlying human relationships. Prayer is not simply an act of worship; it is essentially an attitude of soul which maintains open communication with God and with the spiritual realms. Thoughtful prayer is capable of providing a supply of sustaining power to see us through difficult times in our lives. Prayer and the growth of spiritual understanding lessen the attachment to earthly goods and prestige and enhance our acceptance of God's grace and our awareness of opportunities from the spiritual realm. When you believe that the Spirit of Christ is within you and you look to Him for guidance, you will not walk in fear but have an abundance of faith that He is with you always.

Spirit Guides

We all have spirit guides and some of us have an awareness of them. It is my belief that our spirit guides were at one time also here on earth in the physical reality that we know. It is feasible that some spirit guides may, in fact, be our ancestors, while others may be with us as the result and need of a karmic link. Our guides can hear us when we speak to them and they are with us always for the purpose of helping us. I have a strong awareness of the presence of my spirit guides, but I still have a long way to go, for while I sense their presence, I am not able to hear them clearly. The experience is hard to describe, but I seem to know when I am being guided and I always try to acknowledge their help which is so freely and sincerely given.

Angels

There is a wealth of information on the history of angels in religion and spirituality, and for those who are interested I will provide information on the suggested reading list In brief, the angels in the Christian faith were inherited from Judaism and given greater significance in the New Testament. They are an inextricable component of the Gospel. In Luke 2, verses : 8 - 14, they announced the birth of Christ and told the shepherds where to find the infant Jesus. Angels are always with us and they touch us in powerful yet gentle ways. Belief in communication with angels is one of the rare things that is shared by traditionally conservative Christian groups and the more liberal New Age movement.

It is my belief that we each have a guardian angel assigned to us from the time of our physical birth and I know that my guardian angel has protected me on more than one occasion throughout my life Also, many people who have experienced mysterious assistance, credit their guardian angels for helping them. When you reflect on the events of your life, you, too, may discover examples of angel help. Historically, angels are believed to be messengers from God who bring comfort to us. There are numerous Biblical accounts and other stories of angels helping humankind.

Near-Death Experiences

During my career as a registered nurse I was often privileged to have patients confide in me about their Near-Death Experiences (NDEs). It is not my intention to write about the information given to me by individual patients, but I would like to share some of the insight that I gained about NDEs during my many years of nursing practice in England and in Canada.

Patients descriptions of NDEs contain similar elements:

- a sense of separation from the physical body;

- an immediate release from pain;

- a sense of floating over the physical body or a sense of speeding through a tunnel toward a light;

- a feeling of being loved;

- a detailed review of the patient's life;

- following their return to our physical world, the absence of a fear of death;

- a sense of a new purposefulness in living.

When I questioned patients about the relation between their NDE and religion, the usual responses were that it is important to have a religious foundation as it helps one to understand what is happening, but no one religion is superior to another.

Death and Grief

Medical advances since I first began my career as a nurse have created the potential for a much longer interval between diagnosis and actual physical death than used to occur. Depending on the diagnosis and associated symptoms, such advances can be viewed as a true blessing or as a curse, either of which affect the entire family as well as the dying person. A number of years ago, along with some medical colleagues, a psychologist, and my university research advisor, I did a research paper on the coping mechanisms employed by adult patients diagnosed with acute leukemia. The research findings identified valuable strategies used by patients to handle the emotional roller coaster of remissions and relapses. It is in the context of terminal illness that both the dying patient and the family experience what is known as anticipatory grief .This very complex phenomenon takes into account concerns about the past, the present and the future. While I am not formally qualified to discuss anticipatory grief in detail, I do recall well a young woman, a patient of mine, who was diagnosed with a form of acute leukemia. She knew that the treatment regimen would not cure her, but could extend her life. Earlier when the patient and I had talked together at length about death, she acknowledged her belief in God and in an afterlife, but throughout her illness, her thoughts seemed to be mostly about "going away from her family" and the anticipated and immeasureable loss and grief she experienced as a result of that knowledge. Her concern centered on the present and the future for her youngest child who would be two years old in several months. Her personal goal was to be well enough to hold a very special birthday party for her daughter and I was honoured by witnessing her determination. My patient reached her goal; then, several days later was admitted to the hospital in a crisis situation and died shortly thereafter. One of the birthday gifts that she gave to her daughter was a taped message to listen to when she was old enough.

I have come to believe that death is not our enemy. Our real enemy is disease. As I write these words, a friend is dying of cancer, which in a very short period of time, has viciously spread to several areas of her body. Her enemy is not death, but the lack of bodily function, the insidious pain, and the ensuing loss of dignity. The only reprieve possible is death, which provides the surcease desperately needed after the courageous battle she is currently fighting.

Death is uniquely personal. As a nurse I have witnessed many deaths over the years as well as grieved over the loss of loved ones in my own life Death is rarely, if ever, dignified, but there is a release of the spirit from an injured or ill body that has grown weary from the battle. While I agree that it could be frightening to think that one simply will no longer exist, remember that death is really just stepping from our physical world to the invisible world of the spirit which, some say and I believe, surrounds what we know as earth. Death, then, is really a rebirth, a transition of our spirit to the spiritual realms; therefore, our spirit, which is the very essence of our being, goes on, and so, we actually continue to exist. We are all spiritual beings experiencing a physical existence in this life as we know it to be, but anything physical will eventually wear out, if not eliminated prematurely by accident or design. Death, then, is the only true certainty we can know in life; thus it behooves us to live each moment of our lives with love and to cherish each moment that we are given. Again, I recognize how difficult it is to be continually mindful of living in the now. I urge you to try to keep that thought close to you and to care deeply for all of humanity, for we are interconnected with all of God's creations.

CHAPTER FOUR

STARTLING PYSCHIC EXPERIENCES

uring the early 1990s I travelled to Europe with a good friend for a long-awaited holiday. We often went on vacations together and enjoyed exploring new locations. This particular trip would take us to Frankfurt, a city in Germany that I had not previously visited. We stayed at an absolutely superb hotel located at the airport and the first afternoon managed to drive our rental car to a downtown area of Frankfurt. This jaunt was somewhat of a challenge, but fortunately my friend Maggie has a built-in radar system and is a great navigator. After successfully parking the car we began what would become a four hour walking tour with numerous stops for coffee at sidewalk cafés. The city was alive with music and many interesting people, mimes, jugglers and singers, and it was a delight to be present. There was also a colorful blend of old and new shops, many of them catering to the well–to-do in our society. The streets were clean; people were friendly. All in all, Frankfurt was a spectacular place to start our planned trip to several countries and cities in Europe.

The following morning when we returned to the downtown area we walked over a lovely footbridge, and at the end to our right we saw an archaeological dig. A plaque identified the year the ancient ruin was discovered and other information that I do not recall. Some children were playing in the ruin and there was a lot of laughter from the happy, carefree youngsters. My attention then drifted to a nearby Roman Catholic church, which, I believe, was built in the 14th century and fortunately spared during the wars.

On previous European travels and during the three years that I lived in the United Kingdom, I had been in countless old cathedrals; thus, the idea of visiting yet another ancient place of worship was comfortable but not particularly exciting. Nevertheless, we were there; so why not go in. After we entered through a very large, open doorway and found ourselves in a vestibule, immediately I was flooded with an uncanny sense of familiarity. This déjà vu was accompanied by a deep feeling of awe, of being in the presence of holiness, and I experienced a compelling need to pray. I suddenly felt cold, my skin was covered in goose bumps, and I noticed a distinct and familiar prickling on my arms and the back of my neck.

Everything in me was saying that I need not be concerned about what was happening to me and that in time I would more fully understand what was trying to emerge. I needed to touch the pews, for feeling the wood against my hand provided me with an old comfort, a knowing of something so familiar that it was an innate part of my being. The marble walls, the intricate windows - all seemed to be extremely meaningful, to belong to my life. It was with great reluctance that I left the church and, in fact, after walking one block I turned around and returned, but did not enter because my emotions were in turmoil. I experienced a sense of yearning and tears were rolling down my face. My friend and I went to a nearby café for a drink and discussion in the hope that I would get a hold on myself.   This experience created such a tremendous emotional impact that I still have difficulty trying to verbalize it, as reducing it to words does not even begin to do it justice.

On two subsequent days we returned to take photographs, and each time we visited the church I experienced the same strong feelings of déjà vu and a reluctance to leave. On our final visit a wedding was just about to occur and we were invited to join the others in the church. We selected a pew at the back and felt quite privileged to be there. This final visit created within me poignant feelings, yet a sense of fulfillment and peace, the satisfaction of completing a part of my personal quest to realize the inner design of myself as a conscious being. Today that journey continues, for I recognize that I am still a learner in discovering the interconnectedness between experiences in life, and I try always to be aware of and to consider opportunities for personal growth.

As I write this, I have a photograph of the church by my computer and its presence near me seems very right. I do not quite know what to make of the experience in Frankfurt, but I do know it was real and I think that, in some way, the church is linked to me through a past existence. For most of my life I have been fascinated by the Nazi regime in Germany and I have read many books about the horrific plight of the Jewish population preceding and during the Second World War. Because it is a Roman Catholic Church for which I feel this indescribable affinity, I wonder if I might have been a blonde, blue-eyed citizen of Germany, which in and of itself would have been wonderful; however, I might also have been a Nazi prior to the beginning of the war. I truly do not wish to entertain this latter thought as I have, in my current life, always felt tremendous compassion and love for Jewish people. On the other hand, having experienced past life recall, I am very much aware that one may be a member of any race or creed. I may be able to discover what the particular connection is through a past life regression and I will be open to that possibility when the time is right for me.

As you are reading this chapter, I suspect that you can recall being in a new environment yet feeling as though you have been there before. Also, I anticipate that you have met someone for the first time whom you feel you already know and for whom you may experience an instant liking or disliking. Such feelings of déjà vu are experienced by an amazing number of people, but most of the time we dismiss those feelings as coincidences or mental errors. Another of my surprising psychic experiences involved déjà vu. Prior to starting a particular phase of my health care management career, I attended, as part of my orientation, a number of meetings external to my place of employment. In one such meeting, held in a facility previously unknown to me, I had the strong feeling that I had had the experience before. Listening to individuals and looking about the room for two hours was like replaying a video that I had already seen. The committee members, although I had not met them earlier, were all familiar to me. At the time I puzzled over the experience, but did not share it with anyone as I felt it was just too bizarre. Today, I recognize and acknowledge that perhaps we are not meant to understand all the mysteries of life.

Remarkable déjà vu has struck me on other occasions. My ancestors on my mother's side of the family, the McCallums, originated in Scotland. The first time that I travelled there I was twenty-six years old and living in

England. I have always been interested in genealogy and looked forward to discovering my roots in Scotland. What took me by surprise was the immediate sense of knowing, of feeling completely at home in a country that I had never been to before. In addition, travels in certain areas of Scotland left me with a considerable number of deeply felt impressions of familiarity. The first occurrence I shared in a letter with only my mother. The reason I told her and no one else is quite simple: I knew that she would read with interest my description of impressions, not ridicule me just because she might not have understood my experience, and that she would continue to love me unconditionally. At that time I knew only a handful of people who, in any way, shared my interest in and curiosity about psychic knowing and wanted to explore it.

In subsequent visits to different parts of Scotland, I did not experience the sense of being there before, but whenever I travelled to certain locations, I would feel an almost overpowering sense of being home again. During one such visit after a twenty year absence, I travelled by train from England to Edinburgh, and when I left the train at Edinburgh I was met by a friend and nurse colleague. Again, as in past visits to Edinburgh as well as other places, I encountered a sudden rush of déjà vu that I always welcomed but struggled to describe to others. Over the next few days I stayed in a house trailer located in my friend's backyard. Situated beyond a footbridge at the edge of a Scottish forest, the trailer proved to be an idyllic retreat. My stay there is now one of my favourite memories. My friend, who had recently moved to the area and lived in a renovated toll house (built, I believe, in the mid 18th century), kept the trailer for guests to use. During that visit we talked at length one day about my sense of once having lived in Scotland and concluded that my impression was just a mystery of life. I now understand, since my past life regression experiences, that such an impression can denote an important personal connection. While in the vicinity of and actually in Edinburgh in 2002, I again felt a powerful tug at my heart strings and a jolting sense of déjà vu. I now listen well to such feelings. I truly believe that being open to my psychic energy allows me to trust my intuitive sense, to recognize the true essence of my soul, and to accept mystical happenings that defy logical explanations.

The *Canadian Edition Funk and Wagnalls Standard College Dictionary*, 1978 describes the word psychic: "pertaining to the soul; one sensitive to extrasensory perception; a spiritualistic medium; as well as references to the mind; as being mental as distinguished from physical and physiological." We are all souls and we all have the capacity to develop our psychic abilities which are truly a wondrous gift from God. Unfortunately many of us live our lives at such a rapid pace that we are unable to discern what is going on around us, much less recognize what is going on inside us. I do not recommend in any way that you slow down your life to become lazy (except for the odd weekend), but rather that you take time to evaluate honestly the pace of your life, notice what is going on about you, and focus inwardly to allow yourself calmness in order to create an opportunity to become well-acquainted with your inner wisdom - your intuition. To do this requires tremendous discipline as it is very easy to become totally caught up in everyday events. A passage from the Bible that is helpful to me when I need to reach a calm state is this: "Be still and know that I am God" (Psalm 46: 10). The paths to inner wisdom are many and varied; each one of us must travel his own route.

The following is another psychic experience that I wish to share with you. During most of the 1990s I lived and worked in the large metropolis of Toronto, Ontario. A friend worked in a nearby city and from time to time I would travel directly from work to her place for dinner and a visit. It was customary for me to stay in the guest room and leave in the morning for my drive to Toronto. During this time I was seriously questioning my decision to work in Toronto and thinking earnestly about leaving. One night when I joined my friend for dinner and then stayed over, I went to bed about 10:30 p.m. and read for about a half an hour before drifting off to sleep. At 3:00 a.m. I suddenly woke up to resounding voices saying, "ARLENE THOMPSON, WE LOVE YOU." The voices and the volume were reminiscent of what I had heard when walking down the street in England in 1965. It seemed to me that the noise must have awakened my friend, if not the entire city. I recall getting out of bed, walking into the corridor and standing in the quiet of the night with my hands on the banister. The house was completely dark except for my bedroom light and I stood there for a moment or two. Then I heard the booming voices again: "ARLENE THOMPSON, WE LOVE YOU." This statement was followed by silence and I returned to my bedroom to ponder the message in the middle of the night. I was suddenly very tired, though, and fell sound asleep. In the morning, because my friend and I both had early meetings, we shared only a moment to have cereal and coffee prior to travelling to work. There was no time for much talk, let alone a discussion about my experience during the night. Knowing, however, that it would take me about forty-five minutes to reach my destination, from my car I called another good friend to have a chat and relay my experience to her. I just had to speak to someone about it before I commenced what would be a busy agenda for the rest of the day. Being able to talk about the voices and their message helped me for the moment, and by that evening I was able to consider my experience thoroughly and to conclude that the message was from my spirit guides. Clearly they were supporting me through a difficult time by ensuring that I was aware of their presence and their love. I will also share with you that I thanked my guides that evening for their care, but also requested that if they were to send me that type of message again, to wait until daybreak! On the other hand, I would not have wanted to receive such a message while driving on a busy highway in the middle of the morning rush of traffic. Hearing the voices affected my decision about leaving Toronto and I remained there for another two years. From both a personal and career perspective, it was the best decision.

"Clairaudience" is a term that means clear hearing and signifies the psychic ability to hear voices that are on an energy vibration field not discernible by ordinary hearing. I now understand that clairaudience provides a spontaneous link with a spirit. The first time that I experienced what might have been clairaudience (or perhaps a telepathic message) was in England in 1965; the next time was twenty- seven years later in Canada. On both occasions the voices sounded exactly the same. The echo leads me to conclude that in both instances the messages were from spirits rather than telepathy. You will, I know, understand that hearing the voices again twenty-seven years later was initially somewhat unnerving, even though I quickly realized the message was one of comfort and support and I felt blessed by the connection. If I hear spirit voices again, I believe that I will be much more tuned in as I have learned a great deal about the potential of my psychic awareness, understanding and abilities.

CHAPTER FIVE

UNSEEN POWERS AT WORK

During the 1990s I lived and worked in Toronto, and on a particularly cold but bright winter's day, I began to drive west on the main highway to London. I was approximately 100 kilometers west of Toronto when the weather quickly began to deteriorate. The storm did not really surprise me as that particular area is noted for intense weather, but, I must admit, I hoped for clear road conditions all the way through to London. Before long I noticed several cars pull off the road to wait until it could be ploughed and sanded. I kept driving at a much slower speed, straining to see through the snowy windshield. When I realized how tight my hands were gripping the steering wheel, I made a deliberate effort to relax, but suddenly my car turned toward the ditch. In a split second I resigned myself to losing control of the car and heading over the edge but then an unseen force seemed to place my car back on the road toward London.

I was amazed and grateful. For the balance of the trip, I thanked God, my guardian angel and spirit guides for ensuring my safety that stormy afternoon. I experienced a "knowing" that spirits were with me in the car and would continue to provide protection. The rest of my trip was uneventful and when I arrived in London, I told my family and a friend what had taken place. I still remember, with amazing clarity and a sense of awe, the events of that stormy trip and I have no doubt that I was guided to safety by my guardian angel.

According to the Canadian Oxford Dictionary 1998, the word "angel" is derived from the Old French word "angele" from the Latin "angelus" and from the ancient Greek "aggelos," which means messenger. People from all walks of life have had experiences in which they have been consoled, guided and inspired by angels. I encourage these people to talk openly about their individual experiences rather than dismissing them, for sometimes such events create openings for greater spiritual awareness. Remember these extraordinary moments in your life. You can then build on them intentionally to further your spiritual growth.

During the early 1990s, Elizabeth (the spiritual medium whom I first mentioned in Chapter 2) and I became friends. As she began to know me personally she was no longer able to provide a reading for me . Elizabeth indicated that she seems to block messages for people she knows well such as friends and family members. From time to time, however, while visiting my home, she would spontaneously be given messages from spirits for me. It was during one such time that she said to me, "Arlene, your Mother is here and she wants me to tell you that she is spending a lot of time helping someone that you know. This person lives in Northern Ontario, her name is Mary, and she has a lot of back pain." In 2002 I found out from a relative of Mary that she had back pain during the time period specified and that she eventually had surgery to relieve the constant discomfort. As my mother often went out of her way to help others, it did not surprise me to learn that her spirit continues to reach out and provide comfort to those in need.

During the latter part of the 1990s, as a result of various travels and commitments, Elizabeth and I only managed to keep in touch by letter or telephone during special holiday occasions. As a result of this lack of contact over a seven to eight year span, by the year 2002 she was again able to read for me and I will share the information with you in the next chapter.

In March 2001, I met a medium in Quebec who was highly recommended to me. Her name is Joan and she lives near Ottawa. I will share a selection of the information that she provided to me through use of her clairvoyant and clairaudient abilities. First, though, let me mention that immediately apparent to me was Joan's gracious, caring and sensitive nature. My appointment was for about one hour and took place in her reading room/ office. Two of my friends were invited to watch television in her living room while they waited for me.

After ensuring that I was comfortable and had sufficient paper for taking notes, Joan began her communication with spirits who were arriving to talk to me through her. The following are a selection of some of the messages given to me:

Arlene, you are surrounded with a lot of books and papers that are very important to you and I am being asked to say that you will write a book. You are creative and your heart and your head need to allow you to be creative, for using this skill brings you tranquility. Actually .the spirits said that I would write more than one book. Joan gave me her mailing address and asked me to send her a signed copy! I was told that the first book would be written within two and a half or three years from now and in preparation I would begin to experience more creativity. From a very young age, reading has been my favorite pastime and, yes, I am always surrounded by books. During the time period that I met with Joan, I was involved with a management consultant contract that necessitated my review of many papers. Over the years I have written songs and poetry and I have always found this creative activity to be a welcome respite from the everyday demands of the world. Joan provided another message: Arlene, you are allergic to wasps and this year you must be extra careful to avoid them. I am allergic to yellow jacket wasps and have been since I was stung by one in my brother's yard in the mid 1990s. This incident required me to be transported to the hospital by an ambulance and necessitated a recuperation period at home for two weeks followed by injections of wasp serum each month for the next seven years.

Joan described my residence: *You have your current home in autumn colors, taupe and green, also dark blue. The exterior of your home is red brick with white trim and you have a lot of light from many windows.* My home is decorated in the colors described by Joan with the exception of the exterior trim, and seventeen windows on the main floor do provide a great deal of light.

Joan continued: *The other home you sold is an old one and very special to you; the back yard is like a small park because of its many old trees nearby, flowers and shrubs. That home has a long driveway, a walkway to the front steps and two big trees on either side of the walkway. A man bought your house and he will sell it again within two or three years. You will be moving again. Go with the flow as the change will result in a good investment and you will receive lots of help from a lighter haired person.*

The house that I co-owned from 1979 to 2000 is over sixty

years old. It is a well -maintained one and a half story building in Cape Cod style with yellow brick.

The property does have a long driveway and two large trees on either side of the front walkway. The backyard is as Joan described it and the "park-like" setting was a favorite place for many special celebrations held for family and friends. A man bought the house five days after it was put on the market and I believe he is still living there. At this time my friend and I have no intention of selling our current home, but we keep open minds and are prepared, as Joan relayed, "to go with the flow."

Joan continued with messages for me from spirits:
Arlene, you are a very sensitive person and you seem to have x-ray eyes with your ability to analyze people. You are a very open person with a big heart, a champion of humanity and justice and you are a good teacher. People sometimes take advantage of your giving nature and often you are aware of this and you forgive, but you do not forget. You do not sleep well and you need to have fresh air in your bedroom at night. You like cut flowers in your home, but you do not like plants inside your house. I do seem able to detect quickly someone's personality and I listen well to my intuition as generally I am correct. Friends who know me well have often commented on my thoughtful and generous nature, but I know within myself that there is always room for improvement. Yes, some people have taken advantage of my "good heart" and

I do always forgive. Forgiveness, to me, is born in love, and through an awakening spiritual path I know that dissolving discord and seeking harmony are essential in order to restore wholeness and achieve a deeper understanding of circumstances. When Joan indicated that I do not forget, I believe she is speaking about trust, for when someone has deliberately hurt me in some way, I do not easily trust that person again. Renewed confidence, in my view, must be earned over a period of time. Unfortunately, I do not sleep well at night, and if we lived in a world where I could leave my ground floor bedroom window open, I would be so inclined. Joan was also correct about my preference for cut flowers rather than potted plants in my home.

Joan conveyed another message during our meeting in March 2001:

Arlene, there is someone you care a great deal about who is coming back into your life after an absence of many years. On the first day of April, 2001, I received a telephone call "out of the blue" from someone I do care a great deal about. I am pleased to say that this person continues to be a part of my life.

Everything that Joan communicated to me is meaningful. The way she was able to describe my past and current home lets me know that the spirits of loved ones are aware of decisions and the environment in which I live; in other words, Joan again validated what I sense about spirits being with me, and although, perhaps, I no longer need that validation, it is still really appreciated. The message to write books, I have already "talked" about in "The Introduction" as well as in this chapter, and I will refer to that message again in the next chapter. This first book partially fulfills the prediction I received and validates my attention to well-meaning and loving spirits. In March of 2003, I began to write the manuscript, two years after the first message I received and five months after the second prediction which I received in October 2002.

▼

CHAPTER SIX

❧

Soul Connection

n October of 2002, when I telephoned Elizabeth to ask for a reading, she agreed to see me. It had been over seven years since I last received a reading from her and I looked forward to this appointment. When you read about the messages I received, you will understand that my enthusiasm was justified. I traveled to Elizabeth's home with a friend. We had made arrangements to have lunch after my session. My friend Maggie could have arranged to see Elizabeth for a reading as well but elected just to wait for me in Elizabeth's living room and put in the time by reading the paper.

When I was seated in the comfortable and quiet room that Elizabeth uses for readings, she bowed her head to pray for a few moments. Then Elizabeth began with these words: *Arlene, your mother is here and her spirit is often with you. She is telling me that many spirits are constantly with you, but that part of your problem in not being able to hear them is that you need to separate yourself from the physical world through breathing deeply and through paying attention to meditation that such breathing would create.*

I now pay more attention to my meditation practice in order to allow myself to experience and appreciate the stillness and emerging creativity.

Elizabeth continued with the following: *You have a male guide who is a higher spirit. He was with you before you were born into your current life - you and he were brothers. Also, there is a lady guide here who you knew in the living. She was a big woman who always wore printed dresses and an apron and she is telling me that her name is Alice. Again, I am to tell you that you are getting a lot of guidance from the spirit realm. Your grandmother is close and protective of you.* Before I was conceived, my mother had a miscarriage when she was five months pregnant. The fetus was a male and for reasons I could not understand earlier in my life, I always felt a strong bond with my unborn brother. I now recognize that he may be the male guide and brother that spirits identified to me through Elizabeth. Similarly, from the description and name of the second guide I could easily identify a past neighbor and good friend of my mother. To validate the presence of my grandmother's spirit, Elizabeth described in detail a table which I recognized as the one that used to be in my grandmother's kitchen.

Elizabeth relayed this advice: *A quill is being shown by a writer guide who is waiting to help you with writing. You will have something published. You must write. You must do it. You have had this project on the back burner but now must put it on the front. You should be teaching and talking to people. These activities would be effortless for you and beneficial to others. Moreover, you will meet a woman who will help you to open some of these doors and you will be kept quite busy. I am also to let you know that the timing is right for you to close your current business.* As you know, from having this book in your hand, I have accepted the instruction and encouragement from the spirit realm. Also, at the time of this reading, I was preparing to close my management consulting business. *"There is the spirit of a woman showing herself to me with cancer throughout her body and she is here to be remembered to you."*

Two long-time friends and colleagues died of cancer during the 1990s. While each of them experienced a different primary site and type of cancer, they both fell victim to a spread of the cancer to multiple major organs. I travelled to another province in order to spend some precious time with my friend Belle prior to her death in 1992. During this last visit together over a period of three days, I was struck by how easily we were able to talk about facing death as an inevitable part of existence. The clarity of her unguarded, warm gaze took me quickly back to our treasured camaraderie of youth and discovery. Bless you,

Belle, for letting me see you plainly as you were. Despite a profound sadness in knowing that she would no longer physically be with her daughters and grandchildren, she also knew that death was really entry into another life and she looked forward to being reunited in spirit with her husband. The last time I talked with her on the telephone was about ten hours before she experienced physical death. Later I wrote a poem especially for Belle which her eldest daughter then recreated in needlepoint, framed and hung in her home. In 1901, Hugh Black, a popular preacher in Edinburgh and perhaps in all of Scotland, wrote a wise and wonderful little book entitled Friendship. In 1966 while I was browsing through an antique book store in England, I found a copy which still has a place of prominence on my book shelf. All of my good friends, including Belle, gained an acquaintance with this tattered but delightful book. On page 137, Hugh Black explains that the death of a friend is not really the worst loss one can face; there is a keener grief in having to let go of a friendship. When you think of that concept it is easy to recognize that the former experience softens the heart and leaves memories of love but the latter tends to harden the emotions. From a young age I have believed that one must be a friend in order to have a friend. Trust is a critical requisite for making a friend but many a friendship withers through neglect. I suggest that kindness, loyalty and striving to be our best to our friend provide opportunities for growing in grace, patience and love. I am grateful that, despite distance, time, and diverse interests, Belle and I remained the best of friends and I was pleased to know that her spirit may have been the one to bring a message.

My friend Theresa died in a palliative care home in Ontario. I felt fortunate to have several opportunities to visit with her in hospital and then in the hospice. We always shared a sincere and open friendship with many discussions about death, the spiritual realms and the concept of reincarnation, and these conversations served us well during her short few weeks in the hospice. Visits there were my first introduction to a hospice and it was gratifying to see Theresa being so well cared for by compassionate people. She was encouraged to think of the hospice as her home and she delighted in giving me a tour during my first visit. The memorial service to celebrate her life was held in the hospital where she worked. A poem that I wrote in her memory was read out by the minister and I have included the title and last verse of it for your interest:

My Friend

In that first hour of my last visit you asked me to spend some quiet moments alone with you.

We read a poem; we talked of life, death, pain, family and spiritual beliefs.

We reminisced, laughed, cried and hugged.

Only your eyes, hands, mind and spirit were recognizable as you;

Your body was shrunken with cancer yet bloated with fluid.

Your strength, courage and continuing capacity to care for others, the release of self-consciousness

And the trust that allowed you to sleep told me that you were continuing to grow and change during that final chapter of your personal journey.

Bless you my friend.

I do not know which spirit came to give me a message through Elizabeth, but I have no doubt it was either the spirit of Belle or Theresa.

Elizabeth then went on to say this: *A blonde dog is very happy to let you know that he is able to come through to you and he is wagging his tail very fast to show his pleasure. This dog is letting me know that he passed away about the middle of the year in 2002.* A handsome blonde American Cocker Spaniel, with a warm, loving and good natured personality, belonged to friends. He was a frequent visitor; in fact, he lived in my home for months at a time while his owners were out of the country. He was a wonderful and loyal friend and he is missed by all who knew and loved him. His physical life ended in May 2002.

Elizabeth continued the reading:

There is a woman here who was very close to you and she is telling me that she died in a violent way. She wants you to know that she sends you tremendous love and she is showing me roses for you as a symbol of her affection.. She wants me to tell you that if you go out of this room with nothing else, you must go out of here knowing that she is at peace. She also wants you to know that she does not blame anyone for her violent death. She is telling me that you have a rosary of hers and that you have something else that belongs to her which is kept in a white box and covered with tissue paper or cotton batten. When you open the box she is with you. She says that she is often with you when you are quiet or reading and that you know when she is present. S he says to tell you that she is with her mother and father and that her father's name is Joseph. From 1964 to 2001 I shared a truly great friendship with the person who spoke through Elizabeth. On September 9, 2001, we shared what was to be our last conversation together on the telephone. My friend and her beloved only brother, who was also her dearest friend, died on September 11, 2001, in the World Trade Centre disaster which, as we all know, was caused by a terrorist attack. I received her rosary in the mail a short time after the catastrophe. The family member who sent the rosary knew that it would have a special significance to me. During the days preceding a memorial service in the United Kingdom, the same family member gave me a small white box containing a pair of earrings and a brooch and they were, and still are, covered with white cotton batten. I wore the brooch on my suit jacket when I attended the memorial service. From time to time I do open the box and look again at the contents. The father of my friend was, indeed, named Joseph and he died approximately six years earlier. I am very pleased to have received through Elizabeth my friend's messages and also to have validated my own sense of awareness that her spirit is often with me. The following is something that I wish to share with you. Writing it helped me, as did the reading with Elizabeth, to deal with my grief.

Connections

The day you left was at first an ordinary day or so it was supposed to be,

in our peaceful cocooned existence.

You talked with me only thirty-four hours ago and it was as always, distinctly you, warm and fun-loving, your infectious laughter so easy to recall.

Your world was torn away, unmercifully ruptured, devastated by an unrelenting, contemptuous and viciously depraved evil act.

I knew you were there but I prayed you were not.

My brain constantly rejected the real possibility of your death occurring in such a chaotic, fiery, inconceivable nightmare.

Hours, days, weeks, months and now more than a year past the unforgettable horror of the terrorist attack on the World Trade Centre in New York.

I look for you and though you are not here, you are always close to me.

Sometimes I play a mental game of "remember when," and I promise, as I did before, to keep all our secrets, celebrate your birthday and acknowledge your spirit providing me with your continuous presence in my life.

I miss you, though, in this physical world and it is inconceivable that I am here and you are not and sometimes I think it must be a hoax. I know it to be true though.

You are at peace now, surrounded by love in the spiritual realm.

You are not blameful of others despite the all-consuming evil that caused terror, fear, agony and death in unspeakable ways.

I am not as far along on the journey.

I am learning to trust the discovery of my personal transformation.

As I continue to grow spiritually I have a profound awareness of our continuing connection built on love and friendship.

The reading with Elizabeth continued as she related the following message:

There is a spirit here who is showing himself to me as being tall and very thin. He is saying that he suffered and lingered for a long time prior to his death. He is telling me to let you know that he was very relieved when he finally passed. He mentions being a brother, or feeling as though he were a brother to you and someone else, but the connection is fading and the only other message he sends to you is that April is a time of memory for him. A good friend did indeed suffer a lingering death. His family and friends gathered around him to lend love and support and his partner cared for him day and night for months. I was pleased to receive the message from him through Elizabeth, and while he did not mention the word "peace," I am certain that he has now achieved serenity. I hope that he has also retained his dry sense of humor which we all enjoyed.

Although there were three or four other messages provided to me by spirits through Elizabeth, I would like instead to share the following with you: As Elizabeth was closing her session with me she said, *Arlene, the parents of your friend in the living room are here and they want to give their daughter a message.* I immediately left the room and asked Maggie to go in as her parents had asked to relay a message through Elizabeth. Maggie then received a spontaneous twenty minute reading that was extremely meaningful to her. Following the message from her parents was one from Will, an ex-boyfriend, which validated his presence. Maggie had not seen him for years until she visited him approximately four months before he died. To receive a message from him through Elizabeth was unexpected but accepted by Maggie with a great deal of pleasure. In December, 2002, Maggie visited his widow who was a long-time friend. While they reviewed a number of old photographs, Maggie was struck by one picture of him driving a tractor, an activity which his widow said was something he just loved to do. During the spontaneous reading by Elizabeth in October 2002, part of the message to Maggie was a description of Will happily driving a tractor across beautiful fields, but, at the time, Maggie had no idea of the significance of that description.

The existence of spirits has now become so absolute for me that I am sometimes guilty of forgetting that many people, while they may have a belief in spirits, do not necessarily "know" of spirits because they distrust their experiences just as I once did. I hope that my writings will foster inquiry and the naturally subsequent dawning of awareness, appreciation and valuing of one's own experiences. I have learned to consider myself a student of our universe and I am beginning to have a deeper understanding that we are not physical beings but spiritual beings acquiring experience in a physical world. Every circumstance we are presented with is created to help us with our spiritual journeys and ultimately with becoming the best that we can be regardless of the obstacles and challenges we encounter.

After the 2002 reading that I received from Elizabeth, I invited her to come to London, Ontario for a visit. Just after her arrival on September 10, 2003, while we were talking about a workshop that she had recently attended, she suddenly said, *There is a spirit here who is showing me a large heart-shaped cut-out and asking me to direct it to you with love.* Elizabeth conveyed that the spirit was saying to her that she had actually been trying to get her attention for two days as she knew that Elizabeth was planning to visit me. Finally the spirit just decided to sneak up on her when she least expected it; obviously the spirit was successful. Elizabeth described the appearance of the spirits former physical body and said that she had worked in health care prior to her death. From this information it was easy for me to identify the presence of my cherished friend who had perished with her brother during the infamous 9/11 terrorist attack. She asked Elizabeth to let me know that she is aware of my continuing struggle to accept her violent and sudden death. Knowing that Elizabeth would be visiting me, my friend's spirit knew the time was right for her to communicate again through Elizabeth, to stress to me that she is happy and at peace. To help me to understand what happened, she described her death, the smoke, the fire, the windows breaking. She experienced a terrible pressure on her chest, she could not breathe, she had hurt her knee, it was dark and she was very frightened. She said that two people tried to help her, but she was trapped, could not move and felt a lot of pain. She then described her transition to the spirit world. She said that she became aware of hundreds of spirits arriving to help the victims of the terrible disaster. Her own loved ones were among them to help her through the transition, and then all she felt was love and peace surrounding her. Afterward, she slept for a considerable time to help her soul recover from the devastating trauma. To once again validate her spiritual presence in my life, she then asked Elizabeth to tell me about a birthday which she was not physically here to celebrate. She also conveyed to Elizabeth that she is often with me, particularly in the early hours of the morning. She knows about the ring I received in the mail and agrees that the ring is now where it should be. She showed Elizabeth a large bouquet of bronze chrysanthemums for me. She then said that she knows a lot of people in the physical world and keeps busy checking up on everyone she cares about. She requested that I give her love to another long-standing friend of hers who has a son. She said that I would know who the friend is and through Elizabeth she entrusted me with a special message. The spirit's communication also encouraged me to continue writing my book. Then she simply said, "Blue eyes, blue," before pulling her energy back.

I will offer a few comments on the messages received.

First, it is quite natural for her to present me with such items as a large heart-shaped cut-out to show her love and concern. She would often give gifts to her friends and was a generous and fun-loving individual who also delighted in playing the occasional joke. She had friends in various parts of the world and from all walks of life. I can well imagine that her spirit is kept quite busy checking to see if all is well with those friends she loved. The bronze chrysanthemums may have some significance related to our past travels during the autumn when that type of flower blooms. Outside my front door is a flower bed which currently boasts a very large, bronze chrysanthemum; so reference to the flower may also be another way for my friend to let me know that she is aware of changes in my environment. Elizabeth's description of my friend's physical appearance and the type of work she did validated for me her presence in spirit. It was very difficult for me at the time to hear the message of what she experienced prior to her physical death and tears ran down my face. Maggie, who also loved her dearly, was in the room with us and, sobbing aloud, she abruptly left for a few moments. Then, when the spirit described the love and peace she experienced during her transition to the spiritual realm, I felt the welcoming and wonderful sense that all is now well. This second and purposeful communication by my friend, through Elizabeth, has provided me with another measure of comfort which enables me to continue my personal journey with the sure knowledge that her spirit will forever be close to me and to others within her circle of family and friends. Her birthday was on the 20th of June. At that time, other friends and I gathered for dinner and drank a toast to her with remembrance and love. About two months prior to her birthday I received a ring in the mail that used to belong to her. The friend who was given the ring many years ago wanted me to have it. The message stating that the ring is now where it should be also verifies for me her presence and awareness of all that takes place, and never fails to provide me with comfort. I have no doubt that she is with me, for I am often aware of her presence. I delivered the special message that I was entrusted with and it was received with pleasure and warmth. The content was not at all a surprise to the person who received it and that, in itself, was comforting for her. The message encouraging me to write this book is a continuation of her support that I have received in many ways for years. My friend had blue eyes and her reference to blue eyes, is, I am certain, in memory of our past good-natured and sometimes boisterous discussions about perceived advantages for people with blue eyes.

Only after this second reading did I tell Elizabeth that my friend and her brother died in the destruction of the World Trade Centre by terrorists on September 11, 2001. Until then, Elizabeth was not aware that I knew anyone who perished in the infamous attack.

The next day, September 11, 2003, Elizabeth experienced a vision which she described for me as follows: *A ship is on the horizon, the sun is shining, the water is clear and blue and the ship is sailing swiftly to its destination. Two people are standing at the railing, he tall and fit, and she somewhat shorter. Ruffled by the breeze, her hair frames her face and joy fills her whole being. She is on her way home with the brother she loves and cherishes. They stand next to each other but also apart, their thoughts on those they have left behind. Their journey is of the soul and they have left many whose hearts are heavy with grief, family members and friends, his children and wife now alone. The pair has acquired increased understanding and they are looking forward to their new life without pain or fear as they continue their journey with hope and faith in their eternal existence together. To those they have left behind the message is this: Be glad for them, go on living and growing with the sure knowledge that you will meet again in the spirit realms.*

❦

CHAPTER SEVEN

EVENTS OF PSYCHIC PHENOMENA DESCRIBED BY FRIENDS AND ACQUAINTANCES

I am grateful to the people who have provided me with their stories about psychic phenomena and entrusted me to present the information within this chapter. Some names have been changed but the events are written as told to me. During each of the personal interactions, I made notes of the information provided; later I typed it and gave each individual a copy to ensure that my interpretation was correct.

▪ Elizabeth:

Elizabeth, an international spiritual medium known and respected in several areas of Canada, the United Kingdom and the United States, offers the following comments about her life and practice:

Elizabeth believes that mediums are mediums before they are born. She stated, *"I knew something was different about me right from my early childhood. The stairway in my home had a landing midway and I used to stand on the landing and ' know' that I could fly. Of course I could not, but I believe it was a soul memory from a time when I could".* Elizabeth indicated that she was an unhappy child who did not seem to belong or to fit in and was constantly looking for something but not able to identify it. Her first connection with spirit occurred when she was eleven years old. She apparently liked to walk in the cemetery and read the various gravestones, but at that time was not inclined to talk about the pastime, nor was she really able to understand why she always felt comforted during such visits. She said, *"One day I looked up and I saw a beautiful angel standing at the side of a grave, and although the lady's face was full of sweetness and love, I ran terrified until I arrived breathless at home".* This experience was her first connection with spirit that she is able to remember. Little did she know at the time that she would live most of her life not only seeing, but also hearing and feeling spirit; however, many tumultuous and emotion-laden years would pass before she saw spirit again. She went on with her life, with marriage and children, and when she had mainly fulfilled her responsibility to them, the veil between the spiritual world and the physical world was removed. It was with a great deal of joy and warmth that Elizabeth then stated, *"From that time on, spirits have been my friends, teachers, and companions. I learned that my grandmother had this gift and now two of my daughters and two of my granddaughters also have it. I truly believe that my ability is a gift from God. To be a medium is not an easy life; in fact it is a very difficult one. There are stages when your family does not understand and are often hurt by it and sometimes you lose friends who do not understand. People whom I love dearly have tried in many ways to stop me from doing this work. Many times I have felt tired and thought that I would like to stop and rest and not do this work anymore. I believe, though, that being a medium is something that I agreed to do prior to this current lifetime. I feel that I have made a pact with God and entered a spiritual partnership with my guides and teachers who have always held me up when I have stumbled. With great love and humility I feel privileged to have the gift of communication with spirits in order to help many people".* While all humans possess psychic ability, it is very different from mediumistic talent. As Elizabeth says, *"A medium has the ability to bridge the gap between the spiritual world and the physical world, to act as a telephone between the two worlds. The medium is, therefore, able to access information that proves survival after physical death. By being able to offer such evidence, I have been pleased to assist people through their grieving processes. For instance, when parents are grieving the loss of a child through suicide, they often feel tremendous guilt and they come to see me in an extremely despondent state of mind. To know that the reading has given them proof of their child's survival beyond physical death gives me much happiness. It is wonderful to see joyful tears. While the pain does not go away, it is changed with the knowledge that they were not to blame and that they will see their child again. Still today, in this enlightened age, there are those who say that the work of any medium originates from the devil and not from God. My personal experience however, attests to God's involvement. I have seen marriages saved, and dysfunctional families become functional. Individuals gain a new awareness about their existence; they realize the continuance of their loved ones' presence in their lives and recognize the opportunity to grow and to be the best they can be".* When Elizabeth and I talked in general about why some individuals seek out a medium, she offered her opinion and her common sense approach: *"I think that when people request readings a higher force has guided them to the medium at a time when they most need assistance in their lives. On the other side of the coin, individuals need to recognize that they cannot rely on others to make every decision in their lives for them. A good medium will counsel her/his clients in a way that will help them to become less dependent on both the medium and the loved ones in the spirit world".*

When I asked Elizabeth to provide some final comments, she provided this response: *"I truly believe that I am essentially here as a messenger and that I am one of many who have been so blessed. I wish to encourage those who are just starting out on their journey as mediums to always use their gift for the highest good".*

▓ Kate:

Kate is a management consultant who lives and works in eastern Ontario. She is an animal lover, enjoys sailing and has a great sense of humour.

Kate, a long- time friend, recently reminded me of what she calls "a spooky experience."

She invited me for lunch on a Saturday afternoon. I had had a particularly busy week and was delighted to go out and enjoy a lunch prepared by someone else. Let me tell you about "the Caesar salad experience of a lifetime." Kate, for the first time, made a Caesar dressing and presented me with a huge, superb-looking salad. The odour of garlic quickly permeated my senses, but I thought, what the heck, I like garlic. As it happened we both tried the salad at the same moment and literally gasped in unison with the strength of the garlic taste. The recipe was handwritten and the amount of garlic may have been recorded incorrectly. We have laughed about this culinary moment many times. Kate shared with me during our lunch together (minus the salad) that she is adopted. She confided, *"While I love and enjoy my adopted family, I have always had a compelling need to find my roots."* She had been successful in locating her biological mother who had given Kate a name prior to her adoption. *"What name do you think she gave me?"* Kate asked. Out of the blue a name came to me and without hesitation I said, *"I do not have to guess because your name just came into my mind; your biological mother called you Danielle."* My statement astonished her as that is the exact name that she had been given. I cannot explain how I knew as it just came to me in a flash. I have since, on more than one occasion, met with Kate's biological mother and shared the "spooky experience" with her. Since that conversation over lunch, Kate has studied meditation methods, read many books about psychic phenomena and has increasingly learned to pay attention to her own intuitive abilities.

In a letter Kate described the following experiences: In 1960, approximately three months after Kate's beloved grandmother Muriel died while in hospital in eastern Ontario, Kate was admitted to another hospital. Still grieving over the loss of her grandmother, Kate continued to feel very connected to her and missed her very much. Following the scheduled surgery she had a nosebleed which turned out to be a serious post-tonsillectomy haemorrhage. She remembers the worried looks on the faces of her parents and the attempts of the nun who was a nurse to find a vein to start a blood transfusion. She remembers the doctor trying to insert a rubber tube into her nose and cannot forget the foul odour. Kate's letter continued with these words: *"I recall walking or floating out of the room, but I don't remember if I saw my body on the bed. I was drawn to a bright light just outside the door to the room and I walked down the long, softly lit hallway toward the bright light. I could see a persons's shadow and, intent on approaching, I was calling, 'Wait for me!' I was not afraid; in fact I felt very peaceful. The shadow kept saying to me that I must go back and I remember answering, 'I want to go forward with you.' At the time I must have sensed who the shadow was, but certainly I was not cognitively aware, and I found myself begging to go with the shadow. I was told that I must not follow and when I asked why, I was told that I must stay because my mother needed me. When I woke up, I saw my mother's head on the bed by my side and I remember patting her head and saying to her, I am here. Don't be afraid; I'm okay. My parents never told me that I had been clinically dead, but I have never forgotten the meaningful experience which I had at six years of age".*

In 1981 while Kate was a graduate student at an American university, she made an appointment to have a reading by a psychic who had been recommended to her. At the time of the reading she was twenty-seven years old. During the reading she was asked if she could remember crossing over. At that time she did not understand the term "crossing over." The psychic explained its meaning and asked Kate if she had ever seen a tunnel with a bright light where someone greeted her. Then Kate understood and answered yes. When she was asked if she remembered a particular odour, her response was again in the affirmative accompanied by a snort disgust for the offensive smell. As the reading progressed Kate was asked if she could identify the shadow who greeted her in the tunnel and, when she could not, she was then encouraged to recall her feelings. Kate said, *"Suddenly I realized that the shadow was my beloved grandmother, but I did not voice my realization; instead, I asked the psychic if she knew who it was. I encouraged her to write down the name and said that I would do the same. Another person was called in and asked to read out whatever was on the two pieces of paper. To my delight, both of us had written down the name of my grandmother. I honestly believe that if my grandmother had revealed herself in the hospital to my conscious mind, I would not have gone back to my mother but would have followed my grandmother. What I sensed is that I had a choice: it was my decision to go forward or back, but because of the tremendous love and trust that I felt for the shadow, I chose to follow the guidance given. I would not have willingly hurt my mother, but at the age of six, I desperately wanted to be with my grandmother with whom I felt such a strong connection of love. To this day, I know that she is my angel and I have talked with her ever since that reading"*.

▪ Belle:

Belle was first and foremost a mother. She worked as a Registered Nursing Assistant in hospitals in Ontario and in Quebec. A caring person, she always found time to respond to requests from patients, no matter how busy she was.

I met Belle when she and I worked together at the same hospital. I was in my early twenties and she was a few years older, a recent widow and the mother of two young daughters. Over the years we became great friends and her two daughters were always, and still are, very special to me. Belle was diagnosed with cancer of the bladder which later created metastases in other organs within her body. During 1993, I travelled to a small town in Quebec to spend some time with her. We reminisced about some of the antics of our youth, the fun we had, her daughters, their families, and the special love she had for her deceased husband whom she always missed. We talked of God, of physical death and the dying process. The morning before I left to return to Ontario, Belle asked to speak with me privately, and when we were alone she said, *"Last night my husband came to see me in a dream. He told me not to be afraid as he will be with me to help me cross over."* Then, she said, he held out his hand toward hers and said, *"When the time comes, I will take your hand, so just reach out to me and I will be with you."* In her dream, he also told her, *"You will not leave while our daughters are awake and with you; your passing will occur while they are asleep."* The dream provided Belle with such a great deal of comfort that she decided to share it with her daughters and did so later on the same day that she told me.

After I left, Belle and I talked often on the telephone. It was her wish to experience physical death in her home, but, ultimately, this courageous woman was admitted to hospital where she spent a few short days. Not wanting to leave their mother, at least one daughter stayed in the room all the time. Her youngest daughter shared the following information with me: *"It was about 4:30 p.m. on the day before Mom passed and I was having an internal debate about whether I should go for some supper. Suddenly there was a knock on the door and when I opened it, a woman was standing in the doorway with a tray of sandwiches and some tea. She thought that I might be hungry and since she did not know what type of sandwich I like, she made a variety of them for me. She could see that I was a little hesitant about leaving my mother alone, so she told me that if I wanted to take the tray to the nearby lounge that she would be pleased to stay with my mother, and would page me if anything happened. Even though Mom was comatose, I kissed her on the cheek and told her where I was going and that someone was there with her. I was not gone for very long and when I returned the woman told me everything was fine and that my mother had remained asleep. I thanked her and she left the room. Later, as I was sitting in the chair next to Mom's bed, listening to the sound of her laboured breathing, I fell asleep".* Belle's daughter woke up at 5:45 a.m. and immediately realized that she could no longer hear her mother's breathing. As she gazed at her mother's face she saw a faint smile and a look of peace, and then she noticed her mother's hand reaching out through the bed rails to take her dad's hand just as he had instructed her mother to do in the dream.

A few days later, Bell's youngest daughter went back to

the hospital to thank everyone personally for their help. When she inquired about the woman with the tray of sandwiches and tea, the staff all looked puzzled, and when she described her to them, they informed her that there was no one resembling this woman in the area or on staff. They even called the other hospital units and administration to inquire, but no one had ever seen or heard of her. Upon reflection Bell's daughter became convinced that the kind, sweet woman who provided her with food was an angel. This recognition was very comforting to her, for then she knew that all would be fine.

Belle's physical life ended on February 26, 1994. Since that time, her oldest daughter has told me that she often experiences a dream in which she sees her mother standing near their cabin beside the lake, and hears her mother calling her name. Belle told me on many occasions over the years that she travelled to the province of Alberta to spend time with her oldest daughter, her son-in-law and her grandchildren. The cabin by the lake was a favourite holiday retreat.

■ Renee:
Renee is a popular personal trainer for a well-known fitness club. One day after my fitness training session we had a discussion about psychic phenomena and she told me the following story for inclusion in my book.

My grandfather survived two heart attacks within a one year period. By the way, my grandfather closely resembled the television personality Mr. Dressup, and so that name is what we always called him. I had a dream one night about dancing at a local pub. The phone rang but no one was answering it, and so I ran over to take the call. My mother's voice said to me, 'Renee, I have some bad news; Grandpa died this morning.' This is where the dream ended; I woke up with tears streaming down my face and my fiancé comforting me. Then my telephone rang and it was my mom. She said to me, 'Renee, I have bad news for you ,' and then I finished her sentence by saying, ' I know, Mom, grandpa died this morning'".

■ Tony Avery:

Tony and I met in England in 1964 when we were in the same nursing student class and we have maintained a friendship over the years.

In July 2003, Tony returned to Canada from a long absence when he was living and working in another country. As we were catching up on news, he told me the following events of importance to him. He said that he had visited a psychic in September 2002 and during his appointment with her she had provided him with this information: "In the coming months you will learn about the start of a new life by meeting a girl who will just happen to tell you that she is pregnant. This girl will really not mean anything to you in any way and you will never see her again." The psychic also stated to Tony that his deceased partner would come to him in a dream for the explicit purpose of saying good-bye. Tony   continued, *"approximately two months after my visit to the psychic, I met a new nurse at work who had been sent from another area of the hospital. She mentioned to me that she was pregnant and not able to perform any procedures that involved lifting patients. On that same night I had a dream that a friend and I were packing suitcases to go on a trip. When I asked my partner why he was not packing, he told me that it was time for me to go on my own and that he would not be with me anymore. About a week later while having a discussion with another friend, I suddenly realized that what the psychic had said would happen, did actually happen. While I am a firm believer in the abilities of the psychic that I visited, I was still amazed by her accurate predictions. I am now able to go forward into my future with a firm belief that I have my deceased partner's blessing".*

Tony Avery's story brings to mind the various stages of the grieving process and the fact that we move through those stages at different paces. After the loss of a loved one, we are often in a wave of confusion and wonder how we can go on. There is no set or easy answer for dealing with the physical loss of a loved one, but it helps to recognize that we may be taken by surprise at our responses to such a loss. Bereavement support groups are recommended to help one deal with the shock, denial, anger and despair that are often experienced. With the physical loss of loved ones in my own life, I recall experiencing an indescribable loneliness and a sense of being forever changed. Understanding and accepting your personal grieving and all the feelings experienced are vital to dealing with life after a loss. These requirements include accepting encounters with spirits of loved ones, encounters which many people have but seldom talk about as there is still a taboo attached to belief in such encounters. In August 2003 I read about a research project designed to learn how such occurrences might affect the grieving process. In my personal experience, I always find it comforting to be aware of the spirit presence of a loved one. The encounters, though, however meaningful, should not interfere with the ability to continue with day-to-day activities; nor should they take away our realization of how important it is to live in the present while still cherishing valuable memories.

■ Priscilla:

Priscilla is a nurse, wife, mother, friend and devout Christian.

She had to undergo a magnetic resonance imaging test which is sometimes worrisome to individuals who are nervous about being in a confined area (claustrophobic). Being a reasonable and sensible person, Priscilla listened to reassuring words from well-meaning people, yet still harboured some degree of fear about the actual procedure.

During the latter part of the afternoon on the day of the test she shared the following information with me: *"When the diagnostic process began, I kept repeating in my mind a hymn that I especially like. I did this to calm myself as I knew the importance of having the testing completed. Suddenly I could hear an entire choir, completely surrounding me, singing my favourite hymn, 'The Deep Deep Love of Jesus.' The music made me forget my fear of being confined".* This experience provided Priscilla with comfort and reassurance in the midst of a stressful situation. It seems to me that Priscilla's guardian angel was with her.

▪ Paul:

Paul is a registered nurse who graduated in 1978. He is happily married and the father of two children, a daughter and a son. While he spent many years providing direct patient care at the bedside, he now works as an operating room nurse.

When Paul was twenty years of age, he was involved in a serious motor cycle accident which left him unconscious for over three hours. Upon awakening in the hospital, he was told that he had suffered a mild concussion and then was discharged home with instructions to take aspirin for headaches as required. At the time of this injury Paul was working as a welder with aspirations of becoming a high school teacher in the technical field.

Seven months following the accident when Paul was Christmas shopping with a friend, he suddenly collapsed on a downtown street in the midst of other shoppers. Paul remembers being separated from his body and looking down at himself from the ceiling of the hospital. He watched as numerous physicians and nurses attended to his body. He felt no pain, but was concerned because he saw that his mother was crying and being held back at the doorway by his brother. Then suddenly he was separated from the situation and was flying through a tunnel with brilliant white light. His next memory is of a sudden sharp pain in his chest. Paul remained unconscious for the next twenty-six hours. Throughout this time, his sister Barb stayed by his bedside.

When he regained consciousness he asked his sister, in the presence of his parents and his physician, why his brother Barry had been holding his mother back at the emergency door. His sister was totally shocked by Paul's question. How he could possibly know what had taken place? Paul then explained that, separated from his body, he had watched everything as he floated near the ceiling. He asked why his chest hurt so much and his physician explained that because he had stopped breathing, chest compression and electrical chest stimulation were required as part of the successful resuscitation efforts. The doctor also revealed that Paul had experienced some epileptic seizures which were very likely the result of the accident seven months earlier.

As the result of the neurological damage he suffered in the accident and the subsequent related epilepsy, Paul's life changed considerably. Suddenly he had limited options related to career aspirations or simply the ability to earn sufficient funds on a monthly basis. He was no longer able to work as a welder or to teach welding because the process can stimulate epileptic seizures. He could no longer drive a car nor participate in sports to his usual extent. because of uncertainty about whether his seizures would be sufficiently controlled. These changes caused Paul, who had always been a sports enthusiast and an out-going, involved person, to become somewhat depressed and withdrawn. For a twenty–year-old natural extrovert, this situation was challenging and difficult. He struggled with low self-esteem, embarrassment about having seizures, and the loss of independence.

One day he noticed an advertisement in the newspaper about a four month course to train as an nursing orderly. Paul enrolled partly because he felt that working in a hospital would be a safe environment for a person with epilepsy and partly because, at the time, he had limited career options. During this training period, his clinical instructor assigned him to the care of a young man who had been in a motor cycle accident and, as a result, was a quadriplegic. At the end of the day, the clinical instructor spent some time alone with Paul and talked to him about his attitude and feelings. Paul realized that his teacher had purposely assigned him to that particular patient. He credits her for providing him with an opportunity to change his attitude, accept his own situation, and recognize that things could have been much worse for him. He was hired to work in a busy acute care unit in a major teaching hospital and he remains truly grateful to Eleanor, the nursing manager who demonstrated confidence in him and hired him despite his epilepsy. Paul was suddenly in the right place at the right time in his life for he met Donna, a colleague who inspired him to further his career.

After working for a year or so as an orderly, Paul entered training to become a registered nurse. During the second year of training his class discussed the topic of death and dying, in particular, the groundbreaking book Death and Dying written by Dr. Elisabeth Kubler-Ross, M.D., psychiatrist and author. For the first time Paul realized that he could be comfortable talking about his near-death experience with others beyond his immediate family and physician. This opportunity provided him with a sense of release and joy at being able to talk about an event in his life which carried with it major implications for change.

Following graduation Paul began to work in a neuroscience unit. Again, Eleanor played a part in his being hired as she recommended him to Audrey, another nurse manager who also demonstrated her confidence in Paul by actually hiring him prior to his graduation. Both Eleanor and Audrey touched his heart by taking a chance on him despite his epilepsy.

Working with Donna in the same hospital environment, Paul's relationship with her grew from that of co-worker to friend, and then a defining incident awakened their love for each other. Because of a snowstorm that had crippled transportation within the city, Paul had not been able to have medications that he required to control his epilepsy delivered to him for over three days. During dinner Paul suddenly began to have a seizure. Donna called for an ambulance and accompanied him to the hospital. When Paul woke up Donna was sitting by his bed and he noticed her tear-streaked face. When she saw his eyes open, she alternated between laughing and crying and said to him, *"I didn't realize how much I loved you until I saw you have a seizure."* (Paul had been in a situation known as "status epilepticus," which signifies that many seizures are happening one after the other and is considered to be life threatening). This event was the defining moment in Paul and Donna's relationship, for it demonstrated Donna's love, compassion and support.

Paul's battle with epilepsy successfully ended after four years. Upon reflection, Paul is now absolutely certain that his near-death experience and epilepsy, both of which he initially considered to be major liabilities, have actually contributed to his psychological and spiritual strength. Paul states that he was compelled to learn about neurological nursing because he believed his personal experience would benefit his patients through the care and understanding he could provide for them. Ultimately, the medical field in which he is profoundly interested, the neurosciences, has provided many opportunities for him to listen to patients who suffered from both epilepsy and various brain tumours and to talk about their feelings, coping strategies and concerns related to their prognosis. Paul feels a kinship and a sense of empathy toward patients who are undergoing investigations for epilepsy. He firmly believes that his compassion, patience and understanding have been enhanced as a direct result of his personal experiences. These qualities as well as his marriage to Donna and subsequently his becoming a registered nurse also provided a strong foundation for raising a family. Their daughter Shannon recently graduated as a high school teacher and they are proud of her accomplishments. Their son Ryan, who suffers from a severe progressive neurological disorder, inspires them daily and is their hero.

▪ Dorothy:

Dorothy is a registered nurse currently working in an acute care hospital in Ontario. At an earlier stage in her career she provided patient care at a hospital in Saudi Arabia and also in Bermuda. Dorothy believes that the cultural diversity she experienced has provided her with considerable personal and professional growth.

When Dorothy was having a house built in 2002 the builder notified her that the date for completion was unexpectedly delayed. As a result, Dorothy moved temporarily into her mother's home. It turned out that this unplanned situation of two months duration allowed Dorothy and her mother to get to know each other in a new way. Perhaps they were both able to relate to, respect and like each other as individuals rather than only as mother and daughter.

After working the night shift Dorothy was usually the person who stayed behind in the cardiac care unit to communicate relevant information to the nursing staff arriving for the day shift. Consequently she often arrived home late. One particular morning when the unit was not very busy, her colleagues suggested that she leave early for a change and so she did. After arriving home and entering the house she heard some strange noises coming from her mother's bedroom, and upon investigation she quickly realized that her mother was suffering from a cardiovascular problem. She immediately called 911 and began to perform cardio-pulmonary resuscitation on her mother. Following admission to hospital that morning, her mother's physical life ended as the result of either a stroke or fatal heart attack. In retrospect, Dorothy believes that she was meant to move in with her mother for those two months in order for them to spend some special time together. She does not believe in coincidence, but rather is convinced that everything happens for a purpose, and that while we may not understand the purpose at the time, it is often revealed to us later.

After her mother's death and while she was still living in her mother's home, Dorothy described the following experience to me: She saw an apparition of her mother and heard her voice saying that she wanted her dining room buffet moved. Dorothy was shown that the buffet should sit in front of a window with sheer curtains and that a painting or picture of some ducks should hang to the side of the buffet. Dorothy did not know what to make of this encounter at the time. Dorothy and her two brothers and one sister decided to share the contents of their mother's house among them, the buffet and dining room set was chosen by a brother who was living in Alberta. Several months later Dorothy traveled west to visit with her brother. After she arrived and was being given a tour of his new home, she saw that her mother's dining room buffet had been placed in front of a window with sheer curtains. On the wall to the side of the buffet was a picture of ducks. The arrangement was exactly as described by her mother's spirit at the time of her visit to Dorothy.

During Dorothy's visit with her brother, he indicated that he wanted to locate some additional chairs to match his mother's dining table; so hoping they would find some, together they attended a large antique auction. Unsuccessful and disappointed, however, they decided to leave. Just as they approached the final stall, Dorothy's eyes were drawn to a 1947 Eaton's catalogue and they stopped to look at it. Their parents had married in 1947 and the dining room furniture had been given to them by their families as a wedding gift. Dorothy's brother was delighted to find the name of the manufacturer and photographs of the furniture. His search was over. Dorothy firmly believes that their mother's spirit ensured that they would discover the catalogue.

The next experience that Dorothy shared with me took place in March 2003. During that month she made an appointment with an individual who has the ability to read light fields which she is able to discern around people. For the sake of simplicity, I will refer to her as an intuitive. Dorothy was particularly interested in seeing what the intuitive might be able to tell her as she had been experiencing some unusual happenings. During the meeting the intuitive told Dorothy the following:

- Dorothy experiences visits by two spirit guides named Arthur and Hanna;
- Arthur, described as being practical, helps Dorothy with the handling of her finances;

- Hanna, in contrast, provides Dorothy with nurturing and assists her in being able to nurture others.

Dorothy was able to validate that she was aware of a spirit presence. One of the reasons that she decided to seek a meeting with the intuitive was because she often experienced lights flickering. By this time she was living in her new home and its electrical wiring was up to standard. The intuitive explained to her that when people shed their physical bodies and enter the world of spirit, they vibrate with a much higher frequency which is akin to an electrical field; thus, the flickering lights are a way of saying "I am with you in spirit." This meeting with the intuitive provided Dorothy with some needed clarification and ultimately gave her a sense of comfort.

It was not just traditional but also very important for Dorothy's family to celebrate Christmas together. During the first Christmas after her mother's physical death when everyone was seated at the dining room table, the lights on the chandelier suddenly began to flicker. At that point, they all raised their glasses in recognition of their mother's spirit and proceeded to toast her with love and warmth on that special occasion. Then the lights stopped flickering.

While her brothers, sister and Dorothy were all together, they decided to sort through a considerable number of coins saved over the years by their mother. In the end they agreed not to attempt to sell the coins, but to divide them equally for each to keep. When that decision was reached and verbalized, the lights in the room flickered and it was recognized that their mother was giving her approval of their decision to keep rather than to sell the coins.

The next experience Dorothy described started in the morning after a number of friends had visited her the evening before. Because it was late when her guests left, she decided just to put a bit of soap and water in the wineglasses and leave them on the cupboard for washing in the morning. When Dorothy awakened and went into her kitchen to make coffee, she could hear a dinging noise almost like wind chimes.

On closer inspection, she realized that the fluid in the wine glasses was swirling around and the noise was coming from the glasses. A week or so later when her nephew was talking about the games which he and his grandmother used to play, he mentioned that they would flick their fingers at the crystal wineglasses to hear them ding. Dorothy had been perplexed about the noise from the wine glasses, but after listening to her nephew, she realized it was just another way for her mother's spirit to communicate with her.

Dorothy's mother liked the color pink and particularly loved pink hibiscus flowers. Dorothy, on the other hand, has never liked pink flowers but considers herself partial to deeper, vibrant colors. After getting settled in her new home, Dorothy decided to purchase a red hibiscus plant but it did not do very well. One day when Dorothy entered her home through the garage, she saw an apparition of her mother; two days later the hibiscus was healthy and blooming but the flowers were pink. Another message from her mother!

The following information has to do with repetitive dreams that Dorothy experiences. She often wakes up from a dream in which animals are chewing her feet off. As a consequence she is understandably wary of animals in her current life; so, when she visits her brothers who both own large dogs, she takes a second pair of shoes to wear inside the house. After hearing about her fear, I suggested to Dorothy that she might benefit from seeing a past life regression therapist and I gave her the name and telephone number of Jocelyn in Victoria, British Columbia, whom you have read about earlier in this book. Because Dorothy periodically travels west, she may decide to contact her.

The next two stories are about Dorothy's Uncle George. When he was dying in the hospital, he told his daughter that there would soon be an accident involving some people on their way to work. He also said that no one would be badly injured. At the same time as George was giving his message, a similar one had been recorded on Dorothy's answering machine; the voice sounded like Dorothy's mother's. Two weeks later, one of Dorothy's brothers was in a car accident without serious injuries.

When this same uncle had returned home from a cruise on the Amazon River, he was completely entranced with the absolutely beautiful blue orchids that he had seen while on the trip. When he was dying, his daughter who is also a nurse left her job in California to be with her father. Her colleagues and friends in California sent a bouquet of flowers to her as a gesture of thoughtfulness and she decided to take the flowers to the hospital for her father to enjoy. Among the many blooms were four beautiful blue orchids which delighted and amazed him. After he died, the flowers were placed in the funeral home and then, following the service, wrapped and put in the trunk of the car being driven by Dorothy's cousin. When she arrived at the family home just prior to Dorothy and other family members, she walked up the steps to discover a beautiful blue orchid on the porch. The other four blue orchids were not yet unloaded from the trunk of her car. The presence of this blue orchid on the porch was believed to be a sign of appreciation from Dorothy's Uncle George.

As a result of her experiences, Dorothy has changed. While she has never considered herself a religious person, she now has a renewed sense of faith. She now believes, without a doubt, that our universe offers a world beyond earth that is much greater than our physical, material world. She also recognizes an enhanced spiritual sense which may encourage her to pursue the dedication and discipline of practicing meditation.

▪ Tony:

Tony is a talented artist. He owns a gallery on the east coast of Canada and he hosts two gallery events in Ontario each year. He is also an opera singer and performs with the Orlando Opera Company in Florida.

When Tony was in high school and on his way back from a trip to Niagara Falls with friends, he suddenly experienced a vision of a car accident. The vision was so real that he immediately called out to the driver to stop the car. By the time the driver stopped, Tony's vision had cleared; he realized that he and his friends would see an accident, not be in an accident. Shortly after they resumed driving down the road, they did come upon a collision.

This first vision has triggered more phenomena for Tony. For example, he experiences a strong sense of familiar "knowing" whenever he goes into an antique store or historical site such as Greenfield Village in Michigan or Upper Canada Village in Ontario. What he means by this "knowing" is that he can sense the spirits of the people who either owned the furniture or lived at one time in the area of the historical sites. Sometimes when he enters an antique store, he is almost immediately led to a certain object and then experiences a sense of knowing about the object and person or family who owned it. Tony indicated that at first he found this experience to be confusing and frightening and he would block it out. In the last two decades he has learned to welcome such occurrences and accept them as an integral part of his life.

The following describes a very meaningful event for Tony which took place twenty years ago. Suddenly awakened in the middle of the night from a deep sleep, Tony saw a bright light in the corner of the room. As he began to focus on the light, his body was overpowered by an unseen force and he was not able to move or speak. He was terrified, but then as the light grew brighter, his body and emotions began to relax. When the light totally filled the room, he experienced an overwhelming sense of peace which allowed him to return to a restful sleep. The next morning after talking about the experience to his partner, Tony realized that the pure white light was intended to calm his long standing fear of death. When Tony related the incident to me, he said that he can still recall every detail of the experience. More significantly, he no longer harbours an unnatural fear of death. Tony said that he has always had a strong sense that his grandmother sent this light and its message to him from the spiritual realm. For Tony, this event was the turning point in his search for spiritual meaning.

When he was in grade seven at public school, Tony began to recognize that he has artistic talent. A girl in his class brought in some drawings done by her older sister and, with her permission, he took them home and drew his own versions. When his classmate's sister saw the results, she advised him to keep on drawing. Tony's mother is also artistic and he credits her with encouraging him to develop his skills. By the time he entered high school, he had started to create portraits for his friends. At that time he did not consider art as a career and he entered university with the goal of eventually becoming a teacher. Only after much soul-searching did he realize that his artistic capabilities provided him with the opportunity to pursue a career in which he could freely express his creativity.

Tony firmly believes that he was guided to make use of his innate artistic skills by singing in a church choir for the purpose of serving God .After many years of such service he asked God for a "bigger voice" and he was given the guidance and perseverance necessary to develop that kind of voice. While Tony continued to serve Him in church through music, God granted his request and this "bigger voice" has enabled him to sing opera on a regular basis with the Orlando Opera Company. Without reservation, he joyfully states that this opportunity has added a new and welcome dimension to his life and he considers the gift as His blessing.

With respect to meditation and prayer, Tony said that he prays sometimes, especially in church prior to singing solo. He asks God to help him be centered and calm and he asks for all available angels to surround him with their peace. The angels also help him in other areas. Tony stated, *"Painting, for me, is almost a visual form of meditation and people often comment that my work has an incredible sense of peace about it. I know that the angels play a huge part in my daily life as well as in my artistic endeavours."* He always requests his angels and archangels to guide him. He said *"If I am not sure of something, they will step in and give me a clear message of what to do."* Their answer is in the form of a feeling he experiences, or an actual "yes" or "no" which he can see written as he closes his eyes. He indicated that sometimes, before he even asks, they place the answer before him. He went on to say, *"I have angels appear to me with such a strong presence that they actually lift me up off the ground onto my toes as they seem to pass through me. This experience has happened only twice, and on both occasions I was in a time of crisis in my life."*

In response to my question about whether he has ever had a meaningful psychic experience with respect to music, he provided the following information. When he traveled to Vienna to sing opera, he and his partner visited the site where Mozart is buried. At the gravesite Tony could feel the presence of all the bodies underneath the stone and he could "see" them wrapped in a whitish cloth and covered with a white powder. Then, sometime later while he was sitting on a bench on a cloudy day, he could "see" a horse and carriage and felt that he was in the carriage on his way to a musical concert or formal celebration of dance. Since that time he has had a strong sense of connection with Mozart. He said, *"I have always loved his music; I have performed two of Mozart's operas, The Marriage of Figaro, and The Magic Flute. The words, the music, both conjure up a sense of déjà vu, a strong familiarity and feeling of comfort. I love to paint while listening to his music."* Moreover, Tony maintains that they have determined his vocation: *"My artwork right now is not just a career; it is a ministry set up by God to express the peace and love that we so desperately seek in this world. Many times I am told of just such an effect experienced by people who have chosen my artwork. It is my firm belief that I serve God through all my artistic efforts."*

I shared with Tony some comments that I had written about one of my friends who were killed in the World Trade Centre Disaster, or 9/11 as it is referred to throughout the world, and I asked him for his reaction. In response, Tony wrote the following to me: *"Actually, as I was reading your comments strong emotions began, followed by chaotic images. I believe your friend was the one who initially let me see what had gone on and then it seemed as though I was receiving images from other people as well. I suddenly had a vision of people, some uncannily calm and some very upset, crying, praying and screaming. I could not identify your friend but rather saw many people trying to cope with an unspeakable horror. It was the changes in emotions that were disturbing to me. There were so many to deal with as if each person let out a little of what he was experiencing or feeling. Even as I write this, I can still perceive some of those upsetting images and emotions. Others, however, are more peaceful ones, as what I am seeing now are from some of those people who knew they could not get out but were content to stay and help others. As I let my mind focus on the World Trade Centre, I can feel a lot of unrest from those who cannot yet accept what happened to them. This sense of unrest is partly from those who died and partly from their families and friends. Even from animals, I can sense unrest. It has been my experience, that after I receive new images and emotions, especially wild and unsettling ones, subsequent perceptions are never as intense as the first ones".*

When I asked Tony if he had ever seen an apparition, he described this to me: *"The following experience occurred while I was visiting a church on the west end of Prince Edward Island near Kildare Capes. I was with a friend and we were walking in the cemetery behind the church, facing the sea. I happened to slow down in front of some grave markers that recorded stories about several people who died in a violent storm off the coast in the 1800s. As I read the information, suddenly my body started to tremble with fear. I felt deep sadness and panic. Images of a* dark and cloudy sky along with enormous waves surrounded me. The ground seemed to move beneath me. At this point, I had to shake my head and refocus on something else. When I looked in the direction of the sea, I saw a lady in her mid-thirties wearing a long dress, a double- breasted overcoat, and a very wide-brimmed hat and the high-laced, pointed boots common in that era. The look on her face conveyed the same distress I had felt during images of the storm. Staring at me, she seemed to attach herself to me, in the hope, I guess, that I could help her in some way. When I revealed her presence, my friend cautioned me to be careful and suggested that I try to discover what the apparition wanted. There was however, no clear message, just the staring at me. After awhile, I tried to focus on the walk near the cliffs. My strategy worked until the service in the evening when I looked out of the church window; she was standing outside with the same despairing look. On my way home from the Capes her spirit seemed to be calmer, for it left me. A week later my friend and I attended a service in another old church. I was sitting in a pew where I could see the sea. Once again, without warning, there was the apparition. When I told my friend, she suggested that I ask my angels and hers to request the lady to leave me, to deal with her loss another way. I did as my friend suggested; the angels told the apparition that I could not be of any help to her. That was the end of her appearing to me".

Another time, when Tony returned to his island home after a trip to visit friends and family in Ontario, he encountered a second apparition. *"Arlene, I want to tell you that, after a few days of being here, when I was watching television with my partner and our animal friends, I felt something strange or different in the room. I turned and looked at the piano which was behind me. The orange cat Marmalade was staring at the piano and seemed to have a most peculiar expression on his face. When I looked directly at the piano I could see the outline of an older man dressed in tails and laughing as he played. I felt absolutely no fear with this observation. Instead I felt a real sense of joy because of his happiness. I watched for a few seconds and, as if his playing were a daily occurrence, I turned back to the television. I still strongly sensed his presence, but for some unexplained reason I felt compelled to finish watching the program. His presence lingered for a few hours, but his image faded. Whoever he was, I sensed a strong familiarity with him. The name of a good friend comes to mind, but if the apparition was not him, then it was undoubtedly someone from a past life. Perhaps it was another composer/friend from my Mozart days. I have not seen or heard him since; however, there is a very happy and peaceful feeling in the house. At this point I would like to mention that a friend and I stayed at Tony's house during a visit to the east coast in 2003 and, without reservation, I agree that there is a happy and peaceful feeling in his home".*

Tony then described the following experience: *"Earlier tonight we helped some people from our community church to paint posts and fix gravestones at the cemetery. The church and cemetery are situated on the top of a hill, very near our place overlooking the sea. Anyway, one man was saying that a relative of his (we were fixing his stone at the time) had seen the sinking of the Bismarck. As soon as he said that, pictures of his relative's experiences during the sinking, began to enter my mind. I immediately blocked them out as I knew I didn't have time to focus on what the spirit was letting me see. Receiving images from spirits seems to be happening more frequently than ever before".*

In conclusion I suggest that the stories demonstrate to us that our universe is not impersonal in any way. We are all interconnected and to know the gentle presence of spirits is both humbling and comforting. Mystery is all around us and some of the most fascinating mysteries may never have rational explanations. Throughout the ages however, we have known of people who experienced an unfathomable spiritual connection which transformed their lives. On the other hand, some of us experience a subtle awakening of senses to the reality of the spiritual realm.. Invisible powerful energies are always available to us – listen to your intuitive inner voice.

CHAPTER EIGHT

SPIRITUALITY

When I was a child I lived with my family in a small town in Ontario. Most of our friends and neighbours were immigrants to Canada from various parts of Europe. Many of them struggled to speak English and most of them retained a thick accent or spoke in halting English, what we used to call "broken English". My mother taught me that no matter what people's birthplace or race, they are all children of God; therefore, despite differences in culture, we must accept and respect people and promote understanding and unity rather than prejudice and discord. What a wonderful gift she gave to me. Through her teaching I have easily been able to extend a hand of friendship to others whose lives were often isolated and lonely. If only humanity as a whole could come to the same sort of acceptance, respect and understanding of differences. We would then increase love and compassion rather than hate, jealousy and evil. Instead, we hear continual news reports of rampant killing in America, Iraq, Spain, Israel and Palestine as well as in many other parts of our world. The relentless discord within nations calls for all of humanity to embrace God and to believe without reservation in the fundamental principle that I learned from my mother: each person in the world is a spark of the Divine. Accordingly, the mainstays in our lives should be love, hope, forgiveness, compassion, tolerance and kindness. In order for these values to dominate our thoughts and lives each of us needs a powerful motivation - spiritual guidance. We have only to seek it, for then we receive the spiritual inspiration which comes from only our Divine Source. I cannot recall who coined the phrase "when the student is ready, the teacher will appear," but I do believe it to be true. We need to abandon attitudes carved out of arrogance and embrace humility, for then respect, compassion and the deep understanding necessary for tolerance will follow, despite cultural or religious differences.

During my early years I attended an Anglican church and later a Bethel Baptist church. Through these experiences I began to understand the nature of worship within a traditional religious institution. At the time I did not really comprehend the meaning of fellowship, but for me something was missing. I now believe that authentic fellowship requires faith in our Divine Source, spiritual unity, humility, love, and caring enough to listen well and to speak with candor in a non-judgemental way. Life experiences and my personal spiritual beliefs enable me to recognize that there are many opportunities to share such fellowship and to form an abiding connection with and a love of God without following a traditional religious doctrine. I am convinced that a true sense of spirituality comes from deep within, from a reverence for God and a fellowship with Him which is so great that one is compelled to surrender willingly. Spirituality is such a deeply personal experience that, while many learned people have tried, it cannot be adequately defined. One can only share his individual perspective just as I am doing. I do believe that spirituality is a continuous, evolutionary journey of the soul. Along the way, one acquires a greater understanding of his spiritual being and a liberating wisdom.

When I worked as a nurse during the 1960s in the Eastern Arctic (now known as Nunavut), I began to be aware of a spiritual richness in my life. The remoteness of the tiny village I lived in, the awe-inspiring landscapes, the wonderful and caring Inuit people and their rich culture so different from my personal experience of living in south-western Ontario, all impressed me greatly. I vividly recall my first sighting of the Aurora Borealis; it was well after midnight when I left our small hospital, and as I started to walk, the dark night was suddenly bathed in light. I felt privileged to witness such a miraculous display within God's universe. That magnificent "dance of lights" was the first of several that I recall, but I never lost the sense of awe that it inspired within me. While I did not recognize it fully at the time, those northern experiences contributed to my spiritual growth, for I began to recognize my deep reverence for God and realize a stirring within me to serve Him in some way as yet unknown to me. The almost mystical experience literally brought me to my knees with a sense of absolute bliss and an acute sense of oneness with God. I remember writing a long descriptive letter to my mother on the same night that I first saw the Aurora Borealis, as I just couldn't wait to share the experience with her.

My own belief is that spirituality is an awareness of and openness to God, the universal Energy which guides me along my way in life. My attentiveness to spirit and the work of God's grace in my life is of ultimate importance to me. I recognize that God sets many tests for us, but He also gives us the gifts most necessary to meet those tests which shape our character. During the 1960s I met a nurse in a remote northern area who shared with me the story of her escape from her homeland. Although at first she did not want to leave her parents and siblings, they convinced her that she alone had the best chance to get away from the oppressive life they were forced to lead. With help she eventually arrived in a free, democratic country where she stayed with a compassionate family for one year before immigrating to Canada. While living with this family she was given a Bible, which she continued to cherish as evidenced by the well- worn pages. In her native land, her family was not allowed to possess a Bible, but her parents told the children the Biblical stories that they were able to remember. It was such a joy for her to read the Bible and recognize those stories. She had escaped in the middle of the night, well aware that she would be shot if detected. When I asked her how she had the strength and will to get through the terror-filled hours, she replied that she simply had faith and hope that our Creator would protect her. At the time, I remember questioning myself about whether or not I would be able to summon up the necessary courage if I were in that kind of a situation. Since that time I have met other people who experienced a loss of freedom and endured much physical, psychological and emotional pain, and, without fail, all told me that the only way they were able to survive was through faith and hope in God. I felt privileged by the trust they extended to me and I will never forget any of the people whose lives touched me in such a compelling manner.

The first overwhelming test in my life occurred when I was twenty-seven; my mother died suddenly at the age of fifty-six years, just five days before I was scheduled to return home from England for a holiday visit with her. In chapter one I wrote about my quiet faith and trust in God as He saw me through this terrible storm of loss. Only three weeks later, however, my paternal grandmother died as a result of cancer of the pancreas; I was with her in the hospital when she experienced a massive external haemorrhage and died holding tightly to my hand. When eventually I left the hospital, my clothes still soaked with her blood, I felt terribly alone and totally forsaken by God. The combined loss in such a short period of time created a hurting so intense that words fail to describe it. I remember sitting in my car in the parking lot and feeling absolute spiritual despair, and I truly doubted my will to go on. I did go on, at least outwardly, but unknown to others I felt that I was in an emotional vacuum, a swirling emptiness.

Following my return to England I began to shake off this spiritual malaise, to recognize that I could not possibly continue to deny my connection to, my love for and my faith in God. I needed His closeness, His guidance, His watch over my life. I learned that bereavement is the sharpest challenge to our trust in God and if faith can overcome this heart–rending situation, then truly there is no difficulty that it cannot remove. And faith can overcome profound loss.

One night years after my grandmother's death, my brother was in a semi-comatose state as a result of pain medications and physical exhaustion following a severe heart attack. About 2:00 a.m., his wife, who had been in the hospital for hours, reluctantly accepted my suggestion to go home and try to rest. In my mind I can still see my brother with all the intravenous tubes and oxygen mask and still feel the presence of angels and God's love surrounding him. I stayed with him and I prayed throughout the night for his recovery. During that long watch I became aware of the spirit presence of our mother, father and grandparents; they were there in watchful, loving support of both of us. This experience served to further heighten my sense of privilege in knowing that those we love are always with us. Later in the morning, the physician in charge decided to carry out a procedure known as a cardiac catheterization in order to perform an angioplasty. This medical term describes a method of creating a tunnel-like space in one of the coronary arteries in his heart to allow the blood to flow with less effort and to prevent more damage to his heart. As nurses, his wife and I were both too well aware of the risks involved, the most serious being death as a result of the heart stopping. Knowing, however, he was receiving expert care and that one member of the team was a great friend of mine was reassuring. (That friend is one of the people to whom I have dedicated this book.). We learned later that day that my brother did experience a cardiac arrest during the procedure; in other words, his breathing had ceased and his heart had stopped beating. He had been clinically dead. But the medical team had been able to resuscitate him, stabilize the muscle contractions in his heart and successfully complete the angioplasty procedure. The next day my brother talked to me about his near-death experience. He had felt separated from his physical body and then had become aware of a sense of floating in absolute bliss, knowing a wonderful peacefulness and the absence of pain. Then, suddenly jolted back to awareness of pain, he had heard some of the medical team members calling his name.   As a result of this experience, my brother has no fear of death, for he is certain that after it occurs, peace and love will nourish his spirit. Today he continues to worship God in his private and thoughtful way. A near-death experience brings to mind the words of Psalm 23, verse 4: "Yea, though I walk through the valley of the shadow of death, I will fear no evil: for thou art with me: thy rod and thy staff they comfort me." What could be more daunting than the "valley of the shadow of death" and what could be greater than having such profound faith in God? The words of Jesus make a clear promise: "I will not leave you comfortless: I will come to you," (John 14:18). Many of you have also experienced life situations that confirm the truth of His words.

In the summer of 2000, I discovered a lump in my breast. Within days I received the ominous news that the lump was malignant and that I would require surgery. I felt as though I were in a bad dream and wanted desperately to wake up. When I entered the Regional Cancer Clinic accompanied by my best friend, I truly felt that none of the situation was real, I was not supposed to be there, and all was a mistake! Heart disease has been the major health threat to my family for decades and I had expected to experience one day a fatal heart attack, not cancer of the breast. My friends, family and medical doctor were very supportive and helped me deal with this new reality; however, I experienced an overwhelming sense of sadness and, a devastating realization of my complete inability to control what was happening to my body. After the initial shock wore off, I was eventually able to spend some personal quiet time in prayer and experienced an inner knowing, a reminder that my physical body is just on loan to me and that I am a spiritual being undergoing a physical experience. This renewed awareness allowed me to recognize my continuing connection to God and to all of humanity and gave me an abundance of inner strength to bear whatever I was meant to endure. When I was wheeled into the operating room a month after my diagnosis, I felt a calmness and peace within, knowing that whatever occurred, God was at the helm. I share this experience with you because it is part of our human existence to feel fear, sadness, doubt, denial and sometimes real anger when something happens to our bodies that we cannot control. Turning inward through prayer and meditation helped to quiet my mind, lessen my fear and reinforce my certainty that whatever happens is in God's hands; my part in the process is to trust and to have faith.

Today, as I continue to be treated for breast cancer, I try to live my life with truth, love and compassion. I gladly accept responsibility for my thoughts and actions, for I am sure that the choices I make in this life allow me to learn the spiritual lessons that I am given. Also, I try to live each moment of each day as though it is the only time I have left to live. I admit that I am not always able to be in the present moment, but I continue to try as I believe that goal to be of paramount importance.

The concept of spiritual evolution through a succession of lives which provide many lessons to learn forms part of my spiritual belief system. I also firmly believe that there are no coincidences in life, that there is a master plan for each of us. This idea does not take away free will as we can either flow with the plan or resist it. I have, and sometimes continue to choose both distinct paths, but as I grow in a spiritual sense, then I more often go with the flow and acquire an increasing awareness of my connection to God, the universe and all living creatures within it.

I now know that my time living in the Arctic was intended to happen. It served as the catalyst required for me to seek, explore and question my spiritual path. Fostering this change was undoubtedly the silence of the far north, its slow pace and calm society. For a time I traded the materialistic, demanding world that I knew for a simple existence which encouraged me to contemplate the complexities of life, to look inward, and to communicate quietly with God. Discovering the absolute peace of silence within requires dedication, but the rewards are rich as one learns that silence is a powerful refuge and provides a way to discover intimate knowledge of oneself and the ongoing connection of one's self with God. As Jesus said, "At that day ye shall know that I am in my Father, and ye in me, and I in you" (John 14:20). My love for and connection with God have always been a very private part of my existence. Before this writing I have not often volunteered to share my spiritual beliefs. If, however, my story is helpful to anyone who is searching for spiritual meaning, then I am grateful and humbled. I try to be consistently conscious of God's presence in my life; however, although freely admitting that I still have a long way to go, also rush to say that I am more mindful than I was yesterday and all the yesterdays before. For me spiritual growth is, in essence, a continual journey, available to everyone willing to look within.

For many years after I left the Arctic, I would find myself longing to return. Since I gained an understanding and acceptance of my personal psychic experiences, witnessed the power of prayer, learned the value of meditation, and continue to acknowledge this wondrous journey along my spiritual path, no longer do I experience the yearning, the lingering ache within the core of my being, for now I am aware of the constant presence of our Divine Lord in my life. I know without a doubt that God is the Divine Source of all; He is all powerful, all knowing, and present everywhere. A spark of the Divine Source resides within each of us and the absolute joy of acknowledging our specialness as creations of God is far beyond the power of words to describe.

I feel very fortunate that I enjoy reading. There is a wealth of knowledge available about the need to live in the present and I now try consistently to focus on and be attentive to each moment. For me, embracing the simplicity of truly living moment to moment is a life-long journey that requires tremendous devotion and I am very much aware of my constant struggle to be mindful of each instant. Consider how much of our time is spent thinking of something in the past or wishing for something in the future. It truly takes dedicated mindfulness to stay tuned to and fully present in the now.

Setting aside time for meditation, I discovered, requires considerable discipline, particularly in the early stages. Also, contemplation is a journey taken alone. My commitment to silence, to a profound stillness such as I experience through meditation, is not something I can give to others nor receive from them. It is a private journey not limited to only mystics or saints, but possible for all who pause from their everyday demands to seek silence and wisdom within. This quest is unfamiliar territory for most of us; it is not easy to break old habits of filling our days with busyness. Some people try to fill their every moment with other people either in person or on the telephone. Possibly such silence as is required for meditation may initially prove to be frightening for them. When I began to learn how to meditate, I usually just fell asleep and I thought that I would never be able to reach my goal of inner development. I do not fall asleep anymore and my journey continues!

In summary, God is our Divine Source and this knowledge leads to my belief that He created our world as an act of love, for God is love. Spirituality engages the intimate characteristics of a person; our souls are the sanctuaries of our deepest values. Being spiritual calls for living each moment in the present with conscious awareness of one's relationship with God.

LIFE UNBROKEN

Death is nothing at all—-
I have only slipped away into the next room
I am I—-and you are you—-
Whatever we were to each other, that we are still.
Call me by my old familiar name, speak to me in the
easy way
Which you always used.

Put no difference into your tone
Wear no forced air of solemnity or sorrow
Laugh as we always laughed at the little jokes we
enjoyed to-gether
Play, smile, think of me, pray for me
Let my name be the household word that it ever was;
Let it be spoken without effort, without the ghost of a
shadow on it.
Life means all that it ever meant
It is the same as it ever was;
There is absolutely unbroken continuity.
What is death but a negligible accident?
Why should I be out of mind because I am out of sight?
I am waiting for you for an interval, somewhere very
near, just around the corner
All is well

Author: Canon Scott Holland, 1847 – 1918

Henry Scott Holland was Canon of St. Paul's Cathedral and Regius Professor of Divinity at Oxford.

The above popular passage comes from a sermon on death written by Scott Holland and entitled "The King of Terrors". He delivered it in St Paul's on May 15, 1910.

A Few Last Comments for Readers

It is my hope that you have enjoyed this journey of the mind and spirit with me and with the friends and acquaintances who contributed to this book. I trust that you have found the book to be interesting and I thank you for thinking about its message. As you know, I do not believe in coincidence: your reading of Invisible Powerful Energies was meant to happen. For some of you, the contents may challenge your understanding or may lead you to a new understanding of life, death, religion, spirituality and psychic phenomena. If you are interested in learning how to enhance your own psychic abilities, there are books and other resources available to help you with your inquiries and study. On the final pages of the book you will find a list of suggested titles and Web sites. Your psychic sense is a natural gift from God and can be the most trusted source of guidance in your life. Perhaps the true stories of psychic phenomena contained within this book have helped to demystify psychic happenings and made you aware that we all have the capability to listen deeply to our intuition.

By sharing with you my continual spiritual journey I wish to touch the inner you with love. Do not live your life in fear; rather, awaken to the spirit within you and experience the grace of God in your life. Remember always that Christ is within; we are all His very special creations; we are all interconnected. You never have to walk alone.

BLESSINGS AND PEACE TO YOU ALWAYS.

Arlene Thompson

SUGGESTIONS FOR FURTHER READING

- Blake, Tobin. The Power of Stillness. Novato, California: New World Library, 2003.

- Browne, Sylvia. Soul's Perfection. Carlsbad, California: Hay House Inc., 2000. Burnham, Sophy. A Book of Angels. New York: Ballantine Books, a division of Random House, 1990.

- Chopra, Deepak. The Seven Spiritual Laws of Success. Novato, : New World Library, 1994.

- Choquette, Sonia. Diary of a Psychic. Carlsbad, : Hay House Inc., 2003.

- Choquette, Sonia. The Psychic Pathway . New York: Crown Publishers Inc., 1994.

- Dass, Ram. Still Here. New York: The Berkley Publishing Group. 2000.

- Dyer, Wayne W. There's a Spiritual Solution to Every Problem. New York: Harper Collins Publishers Inc., 2001.

- Dyer, Wayne W. The Power of Intention. Carlsbad: Hay House, 2001.

- Evans,Pamela. Dead As I'll Ever Be. Santa Fe, New Mexico: Crossquarter Publishing Group, 2002.

- Gawain, Shakti. Creative Visualization. Novato: New World Library, 2002.

- Knight, Sirona. The Book of Reincarnation. Hauppauge, New York: Barron's Educational Series, Inc. 2002.

- Nuland, B. Sherwin. How We Die. New York: Published by Alfred A. Knoph, Inc., 2002.

- Roger, John. Divine Essence. Los Angeles, California: Mandeville Press, 2000. Sagan, Samuel. Past Life Therapy for Here and Now Freedom. Sydney, Australia:Clairvision School Foundation, 1996.

- Sargent, Denny. Your Guardian Angel and You. York Beach, ME: Red Wheel Weiser, 2004.

- Stevens, Jose, and Warwick-Smith, Simon. The Michael Handbook. Sonoma, California, 1990.

- Voight, Anna, and Drury, Neville. A Way Forward. Boston: Red Wheel/Weiser, 2003.

- Zukav, Gary, and Frances, Linda. The Heart of the Soul. New York: Simon and Shuster Source, 2001.

Electronic

- Broederlow, Christel. <u>What is Empathy – Understanding Being Empathic.</u> 15 Nov. 2003. http://www.healingabout.comlibrary/uc_empath_021 2.htm

- Early Church Fathers. 10 Oct. 2003 http://www.ccel/org/fathers2/-15k

- Moody, Raymond. 20 Oct. 2003. http://www.lifeafterlife.com

- <u>Psychic Development, Attitudes and Practices to Develop the Intuition, The Psychic Detective.</u> 10 Jan. 2004. http://www.newvisionpsychic.com/magazine/ 697/psychicmt.html

- <u>Reincarnation as Taught by Early Christians</u>. 10 Oct. 2003. http://www.theosphy-nw/theosnw/ re-imo.htm

- Willams, Kevin. <u>The NDE and Religion</u>.12 Nov. 2003. http://www.neardeath.com/experiences/ research06.html

- <u>Mediumship</u>. 15 July 2003. http://www.spiritlincs.com/mediumship.htm

ISBN 1412072425